Raymond M. Smullyan

Edited by Gregory V. Gore

Rambles
Through My Library

Praxis International, Inc.

West Chester, Pennsylvania

If this book is not available locally, order toll free by calling: 1-800-772-9472

For information about quantity discounts write, call or email:

        Praxis International, Inc.
        1343 Green Hill Avenue
        West Chester, PA 19380-3959
        (610) 524-0304
        email: info@praxisontheweb.com
        www.praxisontheweb.com

Printed in the United States of America

First Praxis International, Inc. printing, 2009

Library Cataloging Data
Smullyan, Raymond M.
Rambles Through My Library / Raymond M. Smullyan
   p.   cm.
Includes bibliographical references, index, and twenty-two photo illustrations
ISBN 10: 0-9639231-6-1
ISBN 13: 978-0-9639231-6-5
   1. Life. 2. Literary Collections and Criticism. I. Title

128–dc20

Book and Cover Design by Gregory V. Gore

Contents

Prefatory Ramble   5

Part One: General Rambles

Anecdotes and Tidbits   12
Mad Folk of the Theatre   21
The Princes of English Literature   37
Teaching Literature, Literary Values,
   and Style   64
Book Publishing, Bookselling and Book
   Collecting   77
Literary Forgeries, Swindles,
   Counterswindles, and Magic   109

Part Two: Leisure, Idleness, and Quietude

Personal Observations and Views   122
Late Nineteenth and Early Twentieth
   Century Western Views   129
Ancient Greek and Roman Views   146
Chinese Views   150

Bibliography   168

Index   170

List of Photo Illustrations

Charles Dickens, wife, and sister	11
Helen Keller and her dog, Phiz	14
Helen Keller, Miss Sullivan (her teacher), Mark Twain, and Lawrence Hutton	15
Nell Gwinn in the Epilogue to *Sir Patient Fancy*	26
Dora Jordan as *Peggy*, the country girl	27
George Frederick Cooke as *Richard III*	31
Edmund Kean as *Richard III*	31
Junius Brutus Booth as *Richard III*	32
Samuel Johnson	50
James Boswell	50
A. Edward Newton	81
William Makepeace Thackeray	95
Dr. A. S. W. Rosenbach	99
Bernard Quaritch	106
Mountains and Clouds (attr. Hsia Kui)	121
Agnes Repplier, Charles G. Osgood (standing), and Mr. and Mrs. Newton	135
Early Spring in the Mountains (Kuo Hsi)	153
Landscape (unknown)	154
Landscape (Tzu Yü)	155
Landscape (Wang Tü)	156
Clearing After Snowfall on the Mountain Along the River I (unknown)	163
Clearing After Snowfall on the Mountain Along the River II (unknown)	163

Prefatory Ramble

A prefatory ramble might be defined as a cross between a ramble and a preface. Be that as it may, I live surrounded by heaps and heaps of interesting books—some shelved, some on tables, some on chairs, some on floors—that I have picked up at used book stores—most of them quite inexpensively. Indeed, I picked up a copy of Kant's *Critique of Pure Reason* for 5 cents. When I proudly told this to a logician friend of mine, he replied: "I'm afraid you grossly overpaid!"

I am reminded of Mark Twain's definition of a good library: "A good library needn't have any books. All that is required is that it has no books by Jane Austen."

This, in turn, reminds me of Ambrose Bierce's definition of the word incompossible: "Unable to exist if something else exists. Two things are incompossible when the world of being has scope enough for one of them, but not enough for both—as Walt Whitman's poetry and God's mercy to man."

Now, my library may fail to satisfy Mark Twain's definition, but it contains oodles of gems—many that are little known—that will surely interest those of you who like the sort of things I like. Well, of course; that's pretty obvious, isn't it? (I am reminded of the anecdote of Abraham Lincoln, who, when requested to write an endorsement for a book, wrote: "Those who like this kind of book will find it just the kind of book they like.")

What I should have said is that the gems I have found will probably appeal to those who like the sort of things that I have previously written. Like Lin Yutang, I have found some of my sources in the most unlikely places.

Lin Yutang is a most delightful and sensible author—he is really one of my favorites. I strongly recommend all of his books. One may well start with *The Importance of Living* (The John Day Company, 1937).

In his preface he describes his book as a personal testimony, and makes no pretense of being objective. He says that he would have liked to have called it "A Lyrical Philosophy," but was afraid that doing so might lead the reader to expect too much.

Actually, "A Lyrical Philosophy" would really be quite an appropriate title—his philosophy is indeed a lyrical one, beautifully so!

Lin also considered the possibility of writing his book in the form of a dialogue in the manner of Plato, but in view of the fact that the dialogue form has gone out of vogue, he was afraid that if he did so, people wouldn't read him, and after all, an author wants to be read!

I also love the dialogue form, and am quite upset that it is no longer in vogue. But still I am glad that Lin did not choose that form, because it might have lost some of that lovely rambling quality, but perhaps not, since Lin's idea of a good dialogue is one that is leisurely and extends several pages at a stretch with many detours, and comes back to the original point by a short cut at a completely unexpected turn, which he likens to a man "returning home over a hedge, to the surprise of his walking companions."

That's a lovely idea! I think I will follow that plan, but perhaps without intending to do so. I also love detours!

Like yours truly, Lin loved to buy cheap editions of old authors, many of whose names are obscure, and would baffle many a Chinese professor. Indeed if they knew his sources, they would be astounded and regard him as a Philistine, but Lin prefers "finding a small jewel in an ash can than seeing a large one in a jeweler's window."

I love what Lin has to say about Chinese philosophers: He describes them as dreaming with one eye open and viewing life with love and sweet irony. They also mix cynicism with a kindly tolerance and are seldom disillusioned or disappointed, since they never have extravagant hopes.

I hope I have given you a good feeling for what Lin's book is like. Those who have not read it, have I sold you? If not, then I don't think you will like my book either. If so, then I think you will like my book as well.

Coming back to my book, after the above ramble (which is typical of what you should expect), many of my friends have told me that I have a special knack for finding surprisingly interesting passages, even in authors they have previously disliked. For example, one intelligent musician who told me she hated Thoreau and Whitman was absolutely entranced with selections I read her, and begged me to find some more! I have had similar experiences with Emerson, Samuel Johnson and many others (including Eastern writers). Also, people who told me that they never had any taste for poetry have loved translations of Chinese poetry that I read to them.

And so my plan is to take a tour through my library, record my favorite selections and any thoughts set off by them. Thus, this book will be a combination of anthology, essays, scraps of thought, reminiscences, maybe some autobiography, perhaps some letters—anything will be fair game. I shall not be at all systematic, but hopefully there will be some method in my madness. I shall be like the poet Thomas Gray, of whom Hazlitt said: "He had nothing to do but to read and think, and to tell his friends what he read and thought. His life was a luxurious, thoughtful dream."

And so, I shall tell you what I read and think—at least those things that I believe will interest you.

It gives me particular pleasure to see my favorite selections all in one neat package. Moreover, I wish to express my deepest thanks and appreciation to Greg and Susanne Gore, my publishers and editors, for their tireless and most conscientious efforts in making the book what it is. Never before have I had a more wonderful relationship with any publisher or editor.

Of course, I am writing this book as much for myself as for my readers. I cannot spread myself too thin, and so I can get to only a fraction of my library. But I am hoping to write one or more sequels in the future.

Elka Park, New York

Part One

GENERAL RAMBLES

Anecdotes and Tidbits

I will start with the following fascinating incident: On the wall of a house in Princeton, around the turn of the century, was a cast of Abraham Lincoln before he had a beard. No guest could recognize who it was, except for one—Helen Keller! She felt every feature, wonder and uncertainty expressed in her face; and her fingers dwelt particularly on the lower part of the image, returning thereto and lingering about the chin. Finally, she exclaimed, "Why, it looks like Lincoln!"

I got this remarkable account from the book, *Talks In a Library*, by Lawrence Hutton, (G. P. Putnam's Sons, 1905). The author continues: "It was the first time she had "seen" Lincoln without the hair upon his face...And then Helen said: 'Oh that I could see the bare chin of Grant. So much is expressed in the chin; and I seem to know Lincoln better than I did before.'"

It is interesting the way blind people often use the word "see." I was once in a mathematics class with a blind student—the class was given by a Professor K. About a year later, someone introduced me to the student who said: "Ah, yes; I saw him in K's class a year ago."

This book by Hutton contains a good deal of lesser-known facts about Helen Keller, including some interesting previously unpublished letters. Indeed, the book is full of interesting anecdotes of all kinds and is replete with nice photographs. On the following page is a particularly beautiful picture of Helen Keller with her dog Phiz, inscribed to the author in Helen's own handwriting. Following that is a group picture of Helen, her teacher Miss Sullivan, Mark Twain and the author Lawrence Hutton. Helen knew and loved Mark Twain very much. Hutton has many things to say about Mark Twain, and as we are on the subject, let me tell you some of my favorite Mark Twain anecdotes:

Describing an opera Mark Twain saw in Germany, he said: "I enjoyed it too, in spite of the music!"

Twain once defined the German language as the language in which all the verbs come in the second volume.

About the music of Richard Wagner, he said: "Oh, it's probably not as bad as it sounds!"

To   Uncle Laurence
    With the dear Love
of Phiz and his mistress
May 1902   Helen Keller

Helen Keller, Miss Sullivan (her teacher),
Mark Twain, and Lawrence Hutton

Leaving Twain for a moment, I saw last year a contemporary play that took place entirely in Hell. A visitor was surprised when the Devil told him that Richard Wagner was in Hell. "Of course," said the Devil, "he was a vicious anti-Semite!"

"Hmm," said the visitor, "but he wrote such beautiful music!"

"Oh," replied the Devil, "his music went to Heaven; *he* went to Hell!"

Back to Mark Twain, he once had to give an after-dinner speech at a banquet. Tiredly he arose and said: "Homer is dead. Shakespeare is dead. And I am none too well!"

Perhaps my favorite anecdote is about Mark Twain giving a performance at some club in some hick-town in Maine or Vermont (I forget which). No one cracked so much as a smile! He made his presentation funnier and funnier, but still, everyone wore a total dead pan. He wondered: "Am I losing my touch?" Then during intermission, he overheard various members of the audience discussing his performance, and in one elderly couple, the man said to his wife: "Weren't he funny? Weren't he funny? You know, at times I could hardly keep from laughin'!"

Speaking of Vermont, two Coolidge stories that you may or may not know: Coolidge was once at a banquet and for half an hour said not a word. A young lady sitting next to him said: "Mr. President, I have a bet that I can get more than two words out of you!" Coolidge replied: "You lose!"

Now, that certainly shows intelligence, doesn't it? The other story is that on returning one Sunday from church, someone asked him what the preacher had talked about. "Sin," was the reply. "And what did he have to say about it?" Coolidge replied: "He was against it."

In the preface, I compared Mark Twain with Ambrose Bierce and the definition I quoted of incompossible was from Bierce's *The Devil's Dictionary* (Doubleday, Page and Company, New York, 1911). This book is priceless! Here are some of my favorite definitions from it:

Egotist, n. A person of low taste, more interested in himself than in me.

Lawyer, n. One skilled in circumvention of the law.

Ambidextrous, adj. Able to pick with equal skill a right-hand pocket or a left.

Barometer, n. An ingenious instrument which indicates the kind of weather we are having.

Bore, n. A person who talks when you wish him to listen.

Belladonna, n. In Italian, a beautiful lady; in English a deadly poison. A striking example of the essential identity of the two tongues.

Adder, n. A species of snake. So called from its habit of adding funeral outlays to the other expenses of living.

Hydra, n. A kind of animal that the ancients catalogued under many heads.

Cerberus, n. The watch-dog of Hades, whose duty it was to guard the entrance—against whom or what does not clearly appear; everybody, sooner or later, had to go there, and nobody wanted to carry off the entrance. Cerberus is known to have three heads, and some of the poets have credited him with as many as a hundred. Professor Graybill, whose clerky erudition and profound knowledge of Greek give his opinion great weight, has averaged all the estimates, and makes the number twenty-seven—a judgment that would be entirely conclusive if Professor Graybill had known (a) something about dogs, and (b) something about arithmetic.

Hebrew, n. A male Jew, as distinguished from the Shebrew, an altogether superior creation.

Interpreter, n. One who enables two persons of different languages to understand each other by repeating to each what it would have been to the interpreter's advantage for the other to have said.

Piano, n. A parlor utensil for subduing the impenitent visitor. It is operated by depressing the keys of the machine and the spirits of the audience.

I am reminded of two jokes: The first is the definition of a fugue: "A musical form in which one voice after another comes in and one listener after another goes out."

The second is about a father who was once showing off his little boy at the piano. When the kid had finished playing, the father proudly said to the company: "Well, what do you think of his execution?" One member replied: "I'm all for it!"

Now back to Bierce:

Longevity, n. Uncommon extension of the fear of death.

Decide, v.i. To succumb to the preponderance of one set of influences over another.

Defame, v. t. To lie about another. To tell the truth about another.

Positive, adj. Mistaken at the top of one's voice.

Theosophy, n. An ancient faith having all the certitude of religion and all the mystery of science.

Ultimatum, n. In diplomacy, a last demand before resorting to concessions.

The following definition is not by Ambrose Bierce, but it easily could have been.

Sadist, n. One who is kind to a masochist.

The next three *are* due to Ambrose Bierce.

Nihilist, n. A Russian who denies the existence of anything but Tolstoy. The leader of the school is Tolstoy.

Dramatist, n. One who adapts plays from the French.

Logic, n. The art of thinking and reasoning in strict accordance with the limitations and incapacities of the human misunderstanding. The basic of logic is the syllogism, consisting of a major and a minor premise and a conclusion—thus:

Major Premise: Sixty men can do a piece of work sixty times as fast as one man.

Minor Premise: One man can dig a post hole in sixty seconds; therefore—

Conclusion: Sixty men can dig a posthole in one second.

This may be called the syllogism arithmetical, in which by combining logic and mathematics, we obtain a double certainty and are twice blessed.

Mad Folk of the Theatre

And now, to change the pace, I come to one of my favorite books: *Mad Folk of the Theatre* by Otis Skinner (Bobbs Merrill, 1928), subtitled: *Ten Studies in Temperament.* I have always been very close to the theatre, having done some amateur acting in my young days (and *always* acting in my years as a professional magician) and I have known many actors and actresses, and I say with great pride that they have almost always seemed to recognize me as a fellow spirit! (I am reminded of a lovely saying I read somewhere: "Your true friend will know you in a minute better than a stranger will in a thousand years.") Anyway, Skinner's book is about several English and American theatre people from the days of Charles II through the Victorian period.

Incidentally, I have been told two conflicting theories about acting: One, that the ideal actor imitates the passions perfectly, but does not feel them while acting; the other, that the ideal actor must completely empathize and live the part he is playing. Which theory is correct? My own guess is that both approaches are equally valid, one being appropriate to one type of temperament, the other to the other. Actually, a case will come up later of an actor, acknowledged absolutely as first rate by the author, who certainly *did* live his parts—sometimes in a most bizarre way!

Coming back to Skinner, he says that he holds no brief for looseness of morals and cites the example of Thomas Betterton—a man of "frugality and exemplary conduct who took his art, his profession and his habits very seriously...But nothing in his rigid standards prevented his becoming a colossal figure of the stage in his time."

I spent five or six summers with a group, now the Capitol Repertory Theatre of Albany, New York and formerly the Lexington Conservatory Theatre. Lexington is only a twenty-minute drive from my house in Elka Park, and my wife and I spent an enormous amount of time at the Lexington Theatre (owned by a close friend of ours). We not only went to all their plays, but also saw many of them several times and were allowed to attend their rehearsals, and we attended virtually all of their informal readings. We got to know these people extremely well, and I would say that from the point of view of general morality, they were a definitely superior group. From the viewpoint of what is known as sexual morality (a misnomer, in my opinion) I would say that they were hardly any different from the average people of their age group. Also, in the last three summers, we had the good fortune that the Studio Ensemble Company of New York purchased a large house only a couple of blocks from where we live. In it, they have their summer workshops, where playwrights and actors live and work together and attend various classes and give constant readings of new material, which my wife and I enthusiastically attend. I would say the same about this group as about the Lexington group.

As an aside, I worked one summer as a magician in a sideshow of a carnival. Carnival morality is reputed to be extremely low, but I found this to be totally unfounded!

Coming back to the book, a particularly delightful chapter is "Mistress Nelly"—an account of Nell Gwinn, who was successively street Arab, fish peddler, tavern mountebank, orange girl in the theatre, then Drury's brightest, merriest comedienne and finally mistress of Charles

II, with whom she had two sons. Charles sowed his wild oats in great abundance and had many, many children from different mothers. When someone referred to Charles as "the father of his people," the Duke of Buckingham wittily replied: "Yes, of a good many of them." His numerous affairs were public knowledge, and evidently, rather a source of satisfaction to his subjects. About Nell Gwinn, Skinner says: "To Nell Gwinn, the profane elf of Charles II's Court, I present my profound gratitude. No figure in the story of the stage offers greater opulence of gaiety, fascination, vulgarity and common sense. She was sunshine in dark ways—a fine purgative to the morally bilious Charles."

Nell was extremely well loved by her people. Streets and lanes in England are named after her—likewise sweetshops, tearooms, coffee houses and hat emporiums. According to the author, she was honest, loyal, totally free from hypocrisy and bluntly truthful. One day, hearing a great din outside her house, she flew out to find her coachman kneeling on the chest of a burly unskilled laborer, hammering his skull on the pavement.

"What's this?" she demanded.

"He said you were no better than a common whore."

"Get up, you blockhead! Never fight a man for telling the truth."

Nell stayed with Charles till his last days and outlived him by two years, dying of apoplexy at the age of 38. Her last days were brightened by the thought of her handsome son, the *King's* son, the founder of a noble line, his blood mingling with the best of Britain.

Neither Nell Gwinn, nor the other two actresses—Mrs. Bellamy and Dora Jordan—seemed particularly mad. There is one incident in the chapter on Dora Jordan that I found quite touching: Dora had come to the rescue of a poor widow and her children who had been thrown into prison for a small debt. After being freed, the woman followed and caught up with her as she had taken refuge from a shower under a porch. Pouring out her gratitude, the widow and her children fell on their knees. Dora made light of the affair, slipped a guinea into the woman's hand and sent them away with a word of cheer.

A man stepped out from the shadows of the porch and extended his hand.

Nell Gwinn in the Epilogue to *Sir Patient Fancy*

Dora Jordan as *Peggy*, the country girl

"Lady," he said, "would to the Lord the world were all like thee!"

Dora retreated.

"No, I won't shake hands with you. You are a Methodist preacher, and when you know who I am, you'll send me to the devil."

"The Lord forbid! I am a preacher of the Gospel, but do you think I can see a sister fulfilling His commands, and not offer her the hand of friendship?"

"No, I don't like fanatics, and you won't like me when I tell you what I am."

"I hope I shall."

"Well then, I am a player. I know you've heard of me. I am Mrs. Jordan."

After a moment, "Thy calling matters but little. If thy soul upbraid thee not, the Lord forbid I should. He has given thee a large portion of His spirit."

Oh, if only all clergymen were that nice!

The three "maddest" folk of Skinner's book are the actors, George Frederick Cooke, Edmund Kean and Junius Brutus Booth. Of Cooke, Skinner says, "Of all the strange individuals bred of the life of the theatre, none was more mad than Cooke."

Sometimes, though, his madness, or eccentricity, or whatever you call it, was definitely self-destructive. Skinner relates the following weird incident:

> At Manchester, Cooke had pocketed the four hundred pounds his benefit had brought him that night and proceeded to a public house where he fell into a brawl over politics with a group of taproom loafers. On challenging one of them to fight, the fellow declined, saying: "Nah, Mr. Cooke, you challenge me because you are rich and you know I am a poor man."
>
> "Do I? Then look!" said Cooke, and pulling out his bank-notes he thrust them into the fire.
>
> "That's all I have in the world. I am as you are—and now, damn you, come on!"

I cannot share Skinner's enthusiasm for Edmund Kean—indeed, I found most of the chapter quite depressing. Still, it is definitely worth reading. Now, the chapter on Junius Brutus Booth is probably my favorite chapter of the book! Junius was the *elder* Booth—the father of the actors Edwin Booth and John Wilkes Booth, and was probably the greatest actor of the three. To see how mad he was, he had been known to refuse to die as Richard III, on Bosworth Field, and to attack his *Richmond* so savagely as to back him off the stage, out through the stage door of the Bowery Theatre and to chase him, sword in hand, up the alley to the streets and along the Bowery for several blocks! This, to the great consternation of passers-by seeing the amazing spectacle of two individuals, clad in armor, swords in hand, one chasing the other.

I find this incident one of the most delightful in all theatrical history! That's what I call really *living* one's part!

Incidentally, the book has three fascinating photographs of Cooke, Kean and Booth, each in the role of Richard III. Of the three, Cooke looks the most benign, Kean the most sinister and Booth the most mad!

Another Booth incident you might like (I did!) concerns his failure to arrive at the Boston Theatre for a performance of King Lear. Messengers were frantically sent all over to find him, and he was finally located in one of his haunts, surrounded by somewhat inebriated listeners to whom he was pouring out poetry, Shakespeare and the Bible. He first fought the men who tried to drag him back to the theatre, but finally yielded.

George Frederick
Cooke as *Richard III*

Edmund Kean
As *Richard III*

Junius Brutus Booth as *Richard III*

When he got there, the whole audience was in a wild uproar! Instead of going directly to the dressing room, he burst on the stage yelling: "Shut up! Shut up!" This quelled the commotion for a moment. "Keep quiet!" he cried. "You just keep still and in ten minutes I'll give you the God damnedest King Lear you ever saw in your life."

He then indeed gave a performance that left the audience spellbound.

With all his eccentricities, he was evidently a tender husband and a devoted father to his ten children. He had a deeply devotional nature and to all religions he gave the utmost respect—the Protestant, the Catholic and the Jewish. Though in a letter he said that the Hindu religion was the only one he believed to be at all like the Truth.

It is with sorrow that I leave this lovely book—there are so many good things in it! But I can't linger on any book too long, or *this* book will get too long! However, since I am on the subject of the theatre, I wish to tell you something very interesting I came across in Volume II of Justin McCarthy's book *Reminiscences* (Harper & Brothers, New York and London, 1899). It is from his chapter, "Some Memories of the Stage" and the particular item is about the comic actor, Charles Mathews. I quote:

He had his extraordinary mimetic gifts and his marvelous faculty for acquiring an entirely new face without any assistance from artificial make-up, and in fact he could be as amusing a broad comedian as any other when he wanted to assume the part. But by far the best things he ever did were those in which he relied for the highest force of his comedy on no trick of manner, no oddity of gesture, no buffoonery of any kind; but was able to keep the whole theatre in continuous laughter while still retaining the outward appearance, and movements and manner, of an ordinary Englishman in ordinary society. I have seen Mathews' own company, in some of his quietest impersonations, actually checked in their performance and convulsed with laughter again and again by some indescribable touch of humour brought into play for the first time, so slight that one might think it would have passed over unnoticed, yet so irresistible that it upset the gravity of everyone in the house.

Now comes something quite curious: The author says:

I remember hearing a serious argument once maintained among some authors and dramatic critics on the amazing question whether Charles Mathews was a great artist at all. How, do my readers think, did this curious proposition come to be argued? It came about in this way. Some of the company seriously maintained that Mathews was not an artist because he was just as amusing in private life as he could be on the boards: because it came without any effort to him to be a wit and a humorist, and to rattle off his witty and humorous sayings in a manner that made them irresistibly comic; because he had, in fact, an inborn gift of comedy, and therefore could not be called an artist, inasmuch as he was always the same Charles Mathews in private and in public. I do not present the argument as one calling for grave critical consideration, I only give it as an illustration of the manner in which Charles Mathews was a problem to some of his contemporaries.

I must say that I reacted with intense irritation to that argument! To me, the highest type of genius is precisely that which comes most naturally and is the least studied—just as I believe that goodness that comes spontaneously is better than goodness that is motivated by "obedience to morality." In this respect I am the opposite of Immanuel Kant.

McCarthy next speaks of Mathews' remarkable ability to change his voice, as well as his face and tells the following amazing trick which Mathews once played on a friend named Buckingham: Buckingham had an appointment one evening to meet Mathews not long before the beginning of the performance at the Lyceum Theatre. He went to the theatre and made his way into Mathews' dressing room, but did not find Mathews there; instead he found an old friend, Albert Smith, who said that he was also waiting for Mathews. They shook hands and talked together on various subjects. After a while, however, a certain impatience began to make itself manifest on the faces of both men; each began to wonder what had become of Mathews. Buckingham at last said that he could not wait any longer, at which Albert Smith pulled off his false beard, and there stood Charles Mathews!

The Princes of English Literature

Justin McCarthy's *Reminiscences* is well worth reading in its entirety. Chapter II, "The Princes of Literature," contains lots of interesting material on noted authors including Dickens, Thackeray, Tennyson, Browning, Carlyle and others. The author tells the following funny incident about Carlyle and a friend of Carlyle and Tennyson named *William Allingham*, a poet and essayist, whom the author describes as one of the gentlest and least argumentative people he has ever known. One evening, William was at Carlyle's house when there was a little company gathered together and the talk turned upon an eminent English statesman whose political action was then the subject of general controversy. Carlyle denounced this statesman with even more than his usual energy and launched forth into a denunciation, which allowed of no interruption until it had spent its force. Then Allingham began the mildest expostulation, merely prefacing his intended remarks with the suggestion that after all there might perhaps be something to be said on the other side—some reason to be given why the sentence of the court should not be passed against the arraigned statesman. Carlyle cut him short. "Eh! William Allington," he broke forth, "you're just about the most disputatious man I ever met. Eh, man, when you're in one of your humours you'd just dispute about anything."

This utter unreasonableness reminds me of the following funny incident: A mathematician friend of mine and his fourteen-year-old son were once visiting us, and the father kept on talking and talking, as is his wont. At one point the son made one little remark, upon which the father said in a loud voice: "Who's talking?" The boy replied: "You are, Dad; you've been talking for the last two hours." The father replied: "And whose fault is that?" Then came the boy's brilliant response: "Obviously mine, since I didn't interrupt you."

My favorite anecdote in McCarthy's book (and one which I have read to lots of friends) is about the British politician John Bright. It is most unusual and I will quote it in its entirety.

I had a curious argument once with Mr. Bright on the subject of novels and novel writing. I had written a novel, which was published anonymously and was well received by the reviewers and the public. It came in Mr. Bright's way somehow, and he read it and liked it; and I told him it was mine; and out of this arose the argument. He said to me in his kindly way, "Now you have made a good beginning, and I should like to give you a piece of advice: Make up your mind to write novels all about good people."

I was somewhat staggered at first by this peculiar counsel, and I endeavoured to draw him out a little further on the subject. He told me that he liked the novel I had written, mainly because it was almost all about good people. There was only one bad person in it, and he insisted that it would have been better still of that one bad personage had been left out.

I asked him mildly if he thought the publishers would be likely to care much for a novel all about good people; and he answered me by saying that he felt sure the publishers would come to like anything which was liked by the public. Therein I had to admit that he was probably right; but I asked him whether he thought the public would take much interest in romances which were all about good people. Bright contended that the public would be very glad in the end to be educated up to such a point of artistic morality.

Then he went on to argue that there was quite enough of trouble and distress in life, shadowing and darkening the paths of the most virtuous persons, to give absorbing interest to a story although it did not contain the picture of one single villain from first to last. I appealed to the illustrious examples of men like Walter Scott and Dickens and Thackeray; but he held firm to his purpose that the novels of all these writers would have been so much the better if the villains, male and female, had been left clean out of them.

I spoke of the *Vicar of Wakefield*, and asked him how that story could have been worked out without the introduction of a dash of villainy into it; but he was not dismayed, and insisted that Goldsmith would have made his romance much better and wholesomer reading if the young Squire Thornhill had behaved better and if there had been no trick about a supposed sham marriage.

He went on to say that one reason why he never could enjoy Thackeray's novels thoroughly was that there were too many people in them like Becky Sharp and the Marquis of Steyne. I gently suggested that the novelist was supposed to give some sort of picture of real life; and that as there were undoubtedly bad persons in real life, there seemed to be some sort of excuse for the introduction of bad persons into a novel. The answer was quick and quiet: "The very fact that there are bad persons in real life and that we are sometimes compelled to meet them is the strongest reason why we should not be compelled to meet them in the pages of fiction, to which we turn for relief and refreshment after our dreary experience of unwelcome realities."

I was willing to concede a great deal to the principle that a novel ought to teach a healthy moral—in fact, I think I was willing to go a little farther in that way than my literary and artistic studies of themselves could have inclined me.

But Bright insisted that was not enough or nearly enough; and that after a novelist had tainted our minds by pictures of objectionable personages, it did not by any means satisfy all moral ends that he should bring his virtuous personages to happiness and his villains to condign punishment.

I brought up the subject of one of the most popular novels of the day, a novel excellent of its kind, but which persons of unexalted mind might possibly have described as belonging to the "goody-goody" order of fiction—a novel which I knew was intensely admired by many of Bright's friends, and which I presumed had won his own admiration; and I asked him whether he was prepared to find fault with the authoress of that story merely because she had introduced into it a lady whose conduct was not absolutely blameless. I had hoped that this illustration might have some effect on him: but I found that I was mistaken.

He admitted his admiration for the story, and said that it was much healthier on the whole than most other novels of the day; but he maintained that it would have been healthier and better still if the authoress had left her one offender entirely out of the tale. Then I passed on to speak of great poems, and of course I mentioned Shakespeare and dwelt upon the fact that in his plays there are many personages who, like Iago and Iachimo for instance, must undoubtedly be considered very disreputable persons. Even the great authority of Shakespeare did not compel Mr. Bright to abandon his theory. He frankly admitted that it was a decided drawback to his enjoyment of Shakespeare to be compelled to make even the passing acquaintance of wicked persons like Iago and Iachimo.

Then it occurred to me that I had got him at last; and I turned to his own especial favourite, Milton, and I asked him how he was prepared to champion *Paradise Lost*, seeing that nobody on earth could possible be perverse enough to classify Satan and Beelzebub among good persons. But he was ready for me there, too. He argued that the demoralizing effect of introducing bad men and women into novels, or into poems was because weak-minded readers might be led into admiration for them, and might be filled with a desire to imitate them; whereas if was absolutely out of the power of any mortal man or woman to imitate Satan or Beelzebub. He added, also, that Milton's *Paradise Lost* was a very different sort of work from most of our modern novels—an expression of opinion in which I felt bound to agree.

I confess, however, that I thought there was something highly ingenious and well deserving the consideration of the artistic mind in the principle, which he had been laying down, and the distinction, which he drew between Satan and Becky Sharp. One can imagine a young woman of an ambitious turn of mind and a weak conscience being led away into a desire to imitate Becky Sharp; but the ambition to imitate Satan seems to be beyond the level of the most conceited among us.

Macaulay says that an Italian audience in the Elizabethan age would have regarded Iago and not Othello as the hero of the tragedy; and would have admired Iago's clever cajolery and set down Othello as just the sort of person who ought to be made the dupe of the superior intelligence. But even the most censorious critic of Machiavelli would have hardly accredited him with any serious desire to emulate the doings of Lucifer.

At all events, I have done my best to secure a fair hearing for Mr. Bright's theory about novels and plays. I was not a convert to it; and I have not, so far, tried any attempt to write a novel about good people only: and by that admission I leave it open, of course, to any ill-natured critic to say that I might have made a better thing of it after all if I had ventured on such an experiment. But though I have not made the attempt, others more gifted may be inspired to try the enterprise and to see whether a fascinating novel of modern life cannot even yet be constructed out of the sayings and doings of good people only. It is quite beyond my reach of fancy, however, to imagine what an Adelphi melodrama would be without the figure of a villain appearing anywhere in it.

Now, I would like to try a little game: I'll give you a quote and you see if you can guess whose it is. (Yes, it's someone you have surely heard of.)

When a writer has with long toil produced a work intended to burst upon mankind with unexpected lustre, and withdraw the attention of the learned world from every other controversy or enquiry, he is seldom contented to wait long without the enjoyment of his new praises. With an imagination full of his own importance, he walks out like a monarch in disguise, to learn the various opinions of his readers. Prepared to feast upon admiration; composed to encounter censures without emotion; and determined not to suffer his quiet to be injured by a sensibility too exquisite of praise or blame, but to laugh with equal contempt at vain objections and injudicious commendations, he enters the places of mingled conversation, sits down to tea at an obscure corner, and while he appears to examine a file of antiquated journals, catches the conversation of the entire room. He listens, but hears no mention of his book, and therefore supposes that he has disappointed his curiosity by delay, and that as men of learning would naturally begin their conversation with such a wonderful novelty, they had digressed to other subjects before his arrival. The company disperses, and their places are supplied by others equally ignorant, or equally careless. The same expectation hurries him to another place, from which the same disappointment drives him soon away. His impatience then grows violent and tumultuous; he ranges over the town with restless curiosity...The whole world is busied in affairs, which he thinks below the notice of reasonable creatures, and which are nevertheless sufficient to withdraw all regards from his labours and his merits.

He resolves at last to violate his own modesty and to recall the talkers from their folly by an enquiry after himself. He finds everyone provided with an answer; one has seen the work advertised, but never met with any one that read it; another has been so imposed upon by specious titles, that he never buys a book till its character is established; a third wonders what any man can hope to produce after so many writers of greater eminence; the next has enquired after the author, but can hear no account of him, and therefore suspects the name to be fictitious; and another knows him to be a man condemned by indigence to write too frequently what he does not understand.

Well, do you have any guesses? I read this once to an undergraduate class and they loved it! One of them guessed it was Mark Twain. No, it is not Mark Twain. In case you haven't guessed yet, the following quotation from the same author might make it easier:

It is related by Quintus Curtius that the Persians always conceived an invincible contempt of a man, who had violated the laws of secrecy; for they thought, that, however he might be deficient in the qualities requisite to actual excellence, the negative virtues at least were in his power, and though he perhaps could not speak well if he was to try, it was still easy for him not to speak.

In forming this opinion of the easiness of secrecy, they seem to have considered it as opposed, not to treachery, but loquacity, and to have conceived the man, whom they thus censured, not frightened by menaces to reveal, or bribed by promises to betray, but incited by the mere pleasure of talking, or some other motive equally trifling, to lay open his heart without reflection, and to let whatever he knew flip from him, only for want of power to retain it...

In these latter ages, though the old animosity against a prattler is still retained, it appears wholly to have lost its effects upon the conduct of mankind; for secrets are so seldom kept, that it may with some reason be doubted, whether the quality of retention be so generally bestowed, and whether a secret has not some subtle volatility, by which it escapes imperceptibly at the smallest vent, or some power of fermentation, by which it expands itself so as to burst the heart that will not give it way.

A paragraph later, comes a profound psychological observation:

The vanity of being known to be trusted with a secret is generally one of the chief motives to disclose it.

Well, many of you have now guessed the author—it is Samuel Johnson. When I told my class this (after reading the first selection) one of the brightest girls just *loved* it, and said: "That is amazing! I always hated Samuel Johnson. I had to learn him in English class!"

Ah, yes! *Having* to learn something in class! What could be more deadening? What could be better designed to kill a student's love and interest? And I wish educators would stop using that ghastly word "discipline"! They take the most interesting subjects possible such as mathematics (Yes, it *is* interesting, if properly taught!) and totally ruin it by saying: "It may not be interesting, but it's good discipline!"

I recall once I was just beginning to get a high-school student interested in mathematics when his older sister ruined the whole thing by saying: "Look, Ralph, we all know that mathematics is boring. It's the *discipline* that's valuable!" Now, I'd like to know any high school student who would be sold on any subject by that kind of approach!

A related incident: I once had a radio interview with a high school teacher (maybe a principal). When I was explaining to him why I was interested in mathematical logic, he totally missed the point and said: "In other words, it's for the *discipline* of the subject." Nothing could have been further from my mind, but I remained silent. Later in the program, we came back to mathematical logic and I tried to explain again what was the fascination of the subject. He said: "In other words, what you appreciate is the *discipline* of the subject." Fortunately, (or perhaps unfortunately) I had no pistol with me at the time, so I contented myself with merely saying: "That's not it at all! I happen to be allergic to that word *discipline*."

In one respect, I am like Mark Twain: He was totally against the idea of eternal punishment, except for one person: the inventor of the telephone. And I am against capital punishment, except possibly for those educators who use the word "discipline."

Now, please believe me, I am a working mathematician and I know what I'm talking about: Mathematicians *don't* go into the field because of the "discipline" of the subject; they go into it because they find it so unbelievably fascinating! And that is the simple truth.

Perhaps I am a bit overly hard on those who use the word "discipline." Actually, some people need discipline—or at least self-discipline to get work done. But not everybody does! For example, there are some compulsive, obsessive workers who, if anything, need self-discipline to *stop* working! I suggest that Johnson was a compulsive worker. I think that his saying that only a fool would write for any other reason than to make money—I think this was a pure rationalization. I have every reason to believe that Johnson liked writing more than anything else in life, except possibly good conversation.

The passages from Johnson that I quoted were from his essays in *The Rambler*—Nos. 146 and 13 respectively. I may be unusual in liking his essays at least as well as Boswell's *Life of Johnson*. Despite Johnson's incredible narrowness and stupidity in certain areas, his acumen and brilliant insightfulness into others is staggering. Here are some of my favorite (though lesser known) anecdotes and observations from Boswell's *Life*:

Mrs. Johnson, in whose judgment and taste Sam had great confidence said to him after a few numbers of *The Rambler* had come out: "I thought very well of you before; but I did not imagine anything equal to this."

In Johnson's dictionary, he gave a wrong definition. When a lady asked him why he gave that definition, he honestly replied: "Ignorance, Madam, pure ignorance."

Samuel Johnson by
Sir Joshua Reynolds

James Boswell

Johnson once said:

> Idleness is a disease, which must be combated; but I would not advise a rigid adherence to a particular plan of study. I myself have never persisted in any plan for two days together. A man ought to read just as inclination leads him; for what he reads as a task will do him little good...For general improvement, a man should therefore read whatever his immediate inclination prompts him to...what we read with inclination makes a much stronger impression. If we read without inclination, half the mind is employed in fixing the attention; so there is but one half to be employed on what we read.

Comments: These are wise words! Are most educators aware of these vital ideas?

Johnson continues:

> If a man begins to read in the middle of a book, and feels an inclination to go on, let him not quit it to go to the beginning. He may perhaps not feel again the inclination.

Johnson once said to Boswell: "A desire of knowledge is the natural feeling of mankind; and every human being, whose mind is not debauched, will be willing to give all that he has, to get knowledge."

This is reminiscent of Aristotle: "All men by nature desire to know." Do most of our educators realize this?

Now comes a most interesting insight of Johnson:

> It is not easy to make allowance for sensations in others, which we ourselves have not at the time. We must all have experienced how very differently we are affected by the complaints of our neighbors, when we are well and when we are ill. In full health, we can scarcely believe that they suffer much; so faint is the image of pain upon our imagination; when softened by sickness, we readily sympathize with the sufferings of others.

Johnson once told Boswell that he always felt an inclination to do nothing. Boswell observed that it was strange to think that the most indolent man in Britain had written the most laborious work, *The English Dictionary*.

There were other occasions in which Johnson almost "boasted" of his idleness. I don't believe this was so much affectation as an indication that he really loved his work. I believe that one who really enjoys his work finds work and leisure virtually indistinguishable.

Once Johnson told Boswell that he disapproved of studied behavior: "I never considered whether I should be a grave man or a merry man, but just let inclination, for the time, have its course."

Talking of education, Johnson said: "People have nowadays got a strange opinion that everything should be taught by lectures. Now, I cannot see that lectures can do much good as reading the books from which the lectures are taken."

Comments: I heartily agree! But what would happen to the economics of our entire educational system if this important truth were realized? I'm sure that one day it *will* be realized!

Next I come to what I regard as one of Johnson's great stupidities:

Boswell asked Johnson whether, as a moralist, he did not think that the practice of law, in some degree, hurt the nice feelings of honesty.

Johnson: "Why, no, Sir, if you act properly. You are not to deceive your clients with false representations of your opinion: you are not to tell lies to a judge."

Boswell: "But what do you think of supporting a cause which you know to be bad?"

Johnson: "Sir, you do not know it to be bad or good till the judge determines it. I have said that you are to state the facts fairly; so that your thinking, or what you call knowing, a course to be bad, must be from reasoning, must be from supposing your arguments to be weak and inconclusive. But, Sir, that is not enough. An argument, which does not convince yourself, may convince the judge to whom you urge it; and if it does convince him, only then, Sir, you are wrong and he is right. It is his business to judge; and you are not to be confident in your opinion that a cause is bad, but to say all you can for your client and then hear the judge's opinion."

Now really, Johnson; what's come over you? Do you really believe that if the defense attorney believes the defendant guilty, but convinces the judge of his innocence, then it follows that the defendant *is* necessarily innocent—that the judge is necessarily right and the attorney wrong? Of course it is the business of the judge to judge to the best of his ability, but that doesn't mean that he is always successful in finding the truth! This blind obedience to authority, carried to the point of utter absurdity, is unfortunately typical of Johnson at times.

Sometimes Johnson's irrationality is so extreme as to be actually funny (at least I find it so); as, for example, when he said about the people of America: "Sir, they are a race of convicts, and ought to be thankful for any thing we allow them short of hanging." Boswell was quite disturbed by this and wisely writes: "...the extreme violence which it breathed appeared to me so unsuitable to the mildness of a Christian philosopher...that I was sorry to see him in such an unfavorable light. Besides, I could not perceive in it that ability of argument, or that felicity of expression, for which he was, upon other occasions, so eminent. Positive assertion, sarcastical severity, and extravagant ridicule, which he himself reprobated as a test of truth, were united in this rhapsody." (Good God, I wish *I* could write like that! And this is pure Boswell, not Johnson!) Boswell realized it was hopeless to speak to Johnson further on the matter. (If he had, Johnson would probably have replied: "Let this be the end of the matter,

Sir!"—a favorite evasion of Johnson when he took an indefensible position.)

Now, let's get back to the nicer, wiser and more humorous Johnson.

Boswell writes: "When invited to dine, even with an intimate friend, he was not pleased if something better than a plain dinner was not prepared for him. I have heard him say on such an occasion, 'This was a good dinner enough, to be sure; but it was not a dinner to *ask* a man to.'"

Johnson said about one poet: "As he wrote a great number of verses, he sometimes by chance made a good one, though he did not know it."

Boswell relates that Goldsmith being mentioned, the following conversation ensued:

Johnson: "It is amazing how little Goldsmith knows. He seldom comes where he is not more ignorant than anyone else."

Sir Joshua Reynolds: "Yet there is no man whose company is more liked."

Johnson: "To be sure, Sir. When people find a man of the most distinguished abilities as a writer, their inferior while he is with them, it must be highly gratifying to them."

Comment: I am reminded of a comic I know who says about a friend, with whom he is often seen: "The reason I like to associate with him is that I have an inferiority complex, and looking at him makes me feel good!"

Now comes a very acute observation by Johnson: One day, Boswell spoke to Johnson of his own weaknesses and Johnson admitted that he had them, too, but added, "I don't tell of them. A man should be careful never to tell tales of himself to his own disadvantage. People may be amused and laugh at the time, but they will be remembered and brought against him upon some subsequent occasion."

Speaking once of a dull, tiresome fellow whom he chanced to meet, Johnson said: "That fellow seems to possess but one idea, and that is a wrong one."

Comments: I am reminded of a very unpleasant philosopher I know of whom a bright graduate student said: "He is the perfect example of Plato's idea that evil is a lack! It's not that he is positively evil; he just doesn't have enough good qualities."

About this same philosopher, a bright colleague said: "Everything he says is either obviously true or obviously false."

Next, we come to a good example of Johnson's understanding of reverse psychology: A certain Dr. Taylor commended a physician who was known to him and Dr. Johnson and said, "I fight many battles for him, as many people in the country dislike him." *Johnson*: "But you should consider, Sir, that by every one of your victories he is a loser; for, every man of whom you get the better will be very angry, and resolve not to employ him; whereas if people get the better of you in argument about him, they'll think, 'We'll send for Dr. (Butter) nevertheless.'" Boswell says: "This was an observation deep and sure in human nature." I heartily agree!

Boswell himself was a remarkable person in his own right and has been unduly maligned by several who should know better. His relation to Johnson was always dignified, unlike Eckerman's subservient relation to Goethe. Eckerman is at times so abjectly humble towards Goethe that it is embarrassing; never Boswell towards Johnson! When Hannah More was informed that

Boswell was writing Johnson's biography, she urged him to mitigate somewhat the asperities of his disposition, but Boswell replied: "No, madam, I will not cut his claws or make my tiger a cat to please anyone."

Boswell was unabashedly desirous of literary fame. In the preface of his *Account of Corsica*, he says:

For my part I should be proud to be known as an author; I have an ardent ambition for literary fame; for all possessions I should imagine literary fame to be the most valuable. A man who has been able to furnish a book that has been approved by the world has established himself as a respectable character in distant society, without any danger of having that character lessened by the observation of his weaknesses. To preserve a uniform dignity among those who see us every day is hardly possible; and to aim at it must put us under the fetters of a perpetual restraint. The author of an approved book may allow his natural disposition an easy play, and yet indulge the pride of superior genius, when he considers that by those who know him only as an author he never ceases to be respected. Such an author in his hours of gloom and discontent may have the consolation to think that his writings are at that very time giving pleasure to numbers, and such an author may cherish the hope of being remembered after death, which has been a great object of the noblest minds in all ages.

Another person of that period who made no bones about desiring literary fame was David Hume. Still another was Edward Gibbon, who has the following delightful passage in his autobiography:

I am disgusted with the affectation of men of letters who complain that they have renounced a substance for a shadow and that their fame (which sometimes is no insupportable weight) affords a poor consolation for envy, censure, and persecution. M. D'Alembert relates that, as he was walking in the gardens of Sans Souci with the King of Prussia, Frederick said to him, "Do you see that old woman, a poor weeder, asleep on that sunny bank? She is probably more happy than either of us."

The king and the philosopher may speak for themselves; for my part, I do not envy the old woman. My own experience, at least, has taught me a very different lesson. Twenty happy years have been animated by the labor of my History (*The Decline and Fall of the Roman Empire*), and its success has given me a name, a rank, a character in the world, to which I should otherwise not be entitled. The freedom of my writings has indeed provoked an implacable tribe; but as I was safe from the stings, I was soon accustomed to the buzzing of the hornets. My nerves are not tremblingly alive, and my literary temper is so happily framed that I am less sensible of pain than of pleasure.

The rational pride of an author may be offended, rather than flattered, by vague, indiscriminate praise, but he cannot, he should not, be indifferent to the fair testimonies of private and public esteem. Even his social sympathy may be gratified by the idea that now, in the present hour, he is imparting some degree of amusement or knowledge to his fiends in a distant land, that one day his mind will be familiar to the grandchildren of those who are yet unborn.

An interesting comparison of Gibbon and Johnson was made by George Colman his book, *Random Records*:

On the day I first sat down with Johnson, in his rusty brown, and his black worsteds, Gibbon was placed opposite to me in a suit of flowered velvet, with a bag and a sword. Each had his measured phraseology...Johnson's style was grand and Gibbon's elegant; the stateliness of the former was sometimes pedantic, and the polish of the latter was occasionally finical. Johnson marched to kettledrums and trumpets; Gibbon moved to flutes and oboes. Johnson hewed passages through the Alps, while Gibbon leveled walks through parks. Mauled as I had been by Johnson, Gibbon poured balm upon my bruises...

Gibbon's writing is at times extremely powerful. Here is a sample from Chapter 4, Volume 1 of *The Decline and Fall of the Roman Empire*:

> Of all our passions and appetites, the love of power is of the most imperious and unsociable nature, since the pride of one man requires the submission of the multitude. In the tumult of civil discord the laws of society lose their force, and their place is seldom supplied by those of humanity. The ardour of contention, the pride of victory, the despair of success, the memory of past injuries, and the fear of future dangers, all contribute to inflame the mind, and to silence the voice of pity.

His famous History has strongly anti-religious overtones, which was the cause of much criticism. In a conversation with Johnson, Boswell observed that Gibbon had been an Oxonian, and was remembered there for having turned Papist, and since he had changed several times—from the Church of England to the Church of Rome—from the Church of Rome to infidelity, it would not be surprising if Gibbon becomes a Methodist preacher. Johnson laughed and said: "It is said that his range has been more extensive, and that he has once been a Mahometan. However, now that he has published his infidelity, he will probably persist in it." Boswell replied that he was not sure. (I believe Johnson turned out to be right.)

Teaching Literature, Literary Values, and Style

I now wish to turn to an American author who is not nearly as well known today as he deserves to be—I speak of John Burroughs. He was known primarily as a Nature writer, but I would rather turn to his lesser-known literary writings. I like his volume, *Literary Values* (Vol. X of *The Writings of John Burroughs*, Boston, Houghton Mifflin, 1905) that has an essay in it called "Literary Values" in which he says the following:

> Teaching literature is like teaching religion. You can give only the dry bones of the matter in either case. But the dry bones of theology are not religion, and the dry bones of rhetoric are not literature. The flesh-and-blood reality is alone of value, and this cannot be taught, it must be felt and experienced.
>
> The class in literature studies an author's sentence-structure and paragraphing, and doubtless could tell the author more about it than he knows himself. The probabilities are that he never thought a moment about his sentence-structure or his paragraphing. He has thought only of his subject matter and how to express

himself clearly and forcibly; the structure of his sentences takes care of itself.

From every art certain rules and principles may be deduced, but the intelligent apprehension of those rules and principles no more leads to mastery in that art, or even helps to mastery in it, than a knowledge of the anatomy and the vital processes of the stomach helps a man to digest his dinner, or than the knowledge of the gunsmith helps make a good marksman.

In other words the science of any art is of little use to him who would practice that art. To be a fiddler you must fiddle and see others fiddle; to be a painter you must paint and study the painting of others; to be a writer you must write and familiarize yourself with the works of the best authors. Studying an author from the outside by bringing the light of rhetoric to bear upon him is of little profit. We must get inside of him through sympathy and appreciation.

There is only one way to teach literature, only one vital way, and that is by reading it. The laboratory way may give one the dry bones of the subject, but not the living thing itself. If the teacher, by his own living voice and an occasional word of comment, can bring out the soul of a work, he may help the student's appreciation of it; he may, in a measure, impart to him his own larger and more intelligent appreciation of it. And that is a true service.

Young men and young women actually go to college to take a course in Shakespeare or

Chaucer or Dante or the Arthurian legends. The course becomes a mere knowledge course, as Professor Corson suggests. My own first acquaintance with Milton was through an exercise in grammar. We parsed *Paradise Lost*. Much of the current college study of Shakespeare is little better than parsing. The minds of the pupils are focused upon every word and line of the text, as the microscope is focused upon a fly's foot in the laboratory. The class probably dissects a frog or a starfish one day, and a great poet the next, and it does both in about the same spirit. It falls upon one of these great plays like hens upon a bone in winter: no meaning of word or phrase escapes it, every line is literally picked to pieces: but of the poet himself, of that which makes him what he is, his tremendous dramatic power, how much do the students get? Very little, I fear. They have had an intellectual exercise and not an emotional experience. They have added to their knowledge, but have not taken a step in culture.

To dig into the roots and origins of the great poets is like digging into the roots of an oak or a maple, the better to increase your appreciation of the beauty of the tree. There stands the tree in all its summer glory; will you really know it any better after you have laid bare every root and rootlet? There stand Chaucer, Shakespeare, Dante, and Homer. Read them, give yourself to them, and master them if you are man enough.

The poets are not to be analyzed, they are to be enjoyed; they are not to be studied, but to be loved; they are not for knowledge, but for culture—to enhance our appreciation of life and our mastery over its elements. All the mere facts about a poet's work are as chaff compared with the appreciation of one fine line or fine sentence. Why study a great poet at all after the manner of the dissecting-room? Why not rather seek to make the acquaintance of his living soul and to feel its power.

It is such a pleasure to see one's own ideas expressed better than one can express them him or herself, and the above ideas of Burroughs are mine exactly! Likewise with his ideas in the third essay of the same volume—the essay called "Style and the Man." Here is a montage of some of the chief ideas:

I once overheard a lady say to a popular author, "What I most admire about your books is their fine style." "But I never think about style," was the reply. "I know you don't," said his admirer, "and that is why I like it so much."

This is Burroughs' main idea—that style should not be something added, but should automatically emerge from the ideas themselves. He says:

Frederic Harrison, in a recent address on style, is cautious in recommending the young writer to take thought of his style. Let him rather take thought of what he has to say; in turning his ideal values into the coin of current speech he will have an exercise in style. If he has no ideal values, then is literature barred to him. Let him cultivate his sensibilities, make himself, if possible, more quickly responsive to life and nature about him; let him try to see more clearly and feel more keenly, and connect his vocabulary with his most radical and spontaneous self. Style can never come from the outside—from consciously seeking it by imitating the manner of favorite authors. It comes, if at all, like the bloom upon fruit, or the glow of health upon the cheek, from an inner essential harmony and felicity.

There is a good deal of wisdom in Voltaire's saying that "all styles are good that are not tiresome"...In keeping with this dictum is the remark I heard concerning a certain living writer, namely, that he had the best style in literature today because one could read fifty pages of his and not know that one was reading at all; it was pure expression—offered no resistance. This offering no resistance, this ease and limpidity—a getting rid of all friction in the written page—herein certainly lies the secret of much that is winsome in literature...Is not friction to be got rid of as far as possible in all departments of life? One does not want his shoes to pinch, nor his coat to bind; neither does he want to waste any strength on involved sentences, or on cryptic language.

Boy, I can see why Burroughs doesn't like Henry James! Speak of involved sentences! But I guess there are those who like that sort of thing, and they should find it just the sort of thing they like (thanks to Abe Lincoln).

To continue with Burroughs:

The great success in writing is to get language out of the way and to put your mind directly to the reader's, so that there is no veil of words between you. If the reader is preoccupied with your words, if they court his attention or cloud his vision, to that extent is the communication imperfect. In some of Swinburne's poems there is often such a din and echo of rhyme and alliteration that it is almost impossible to hear what the man is really saying.

A bit later, Burroughs says:

But has not style a value in and of itself? As in the case of light, its value is in the revelation it makes. Its value is to conceal itself, to lose itself in the matter. If humility, or self-denial, or any of the virtues becomes conscious of itself and claims credit for its own sake, does it not that moment fall from grace?

I agree with Burroughs about ninety-five percent. The only difference is that I believe that style *perceived as good style* does have a certain value and attractiveness of its own, though I thoroughly agree with Burroughs that in the very best writing, one is not aware of any style. There is something about style, when perceived as style that is a little bit arty, whereas the greatest writing seems artless, and hence is the more artistic. Yes, I believe true art seems artless.

In Burroughs' Journals he says: "The first step which a man or a people takes towards culture is a love of the artificial, as such, while the last and crowning step is a love of the natural and simple."

In another Journal entry, he writes:

Pride of style in writing is just as bad as pride of style in dress, or equipage. The best style is the absence of style, or of all conscious style.

Burroughs' Journals contain some of his best writings. In general, I believe one's journals to be a better indication of the real person than the things written explicitly for the public. I shall now turn to the Journals. (My source is

The Heart of Burroughs' Journals, edited by Clara Barrus, Houghton Mifflin Company, 1928). First some of the lighter entries:

> *Feb. 26, 1878* - I take it as a great compliment when my friends, those who have known me longest and best, say of my writings, "They sound just like you; I see you in every page."

Comment: This really struck a bell with me, since my own experiences have been so similar! So many people who know me have told me that in reading some of my writings, they can hear the tone of my voice, as if I were present. I also regard this as a compliment.

Some writers have this quality and others, equally good, if not better, do not. I wish I could analyze just what causes this!

> *March 26, 1878* - Could I have known, twenty years ago, all the good things that were in store for me, I should have been spoiled. My writing has brought me more fame and money than I ever dared to hope. For the past fifteen years I have had a good income.

Comment: I have been "half" as fortunate. My writings have brought me as much appreciation and excellent reviews as could be desired, but not as much money as I believe they deserve.

> *Oct. 8, 1916* - I find that the editing of my Mss. tires me more than the writing of them. There is something exhilarating in the original writing, but editing is a drudgery.

Comment: Obviously!

> *Oct. 1, 1887* - Great men are not much more likely to be right in their opinions than little men. What absurd beliefs and views of things truly great men have at times! Their greatness is not so much in this as in their power, their grasp, their capacity to master and absorb a multitude of things. Of course I mean opinions upon abstruse or theological questions. In practical, verifiable matters the great man is nearer the truth.

Comment: I'm not so sure that in practical, verifiable matters the great man is nearer the truth!

> *Nov. 13, 1892* - The voice of a multitude is more impressive than the separate voices of the individuals composing the multitude. There is a spirit and an atmosphere that individual trees hardly hint. Is the social organism a real entity? Is there a general will over or under all the private wills? The country speaks—how pompous,

how commanding! No doubt our imaginations have much to do with it.

Comment: None

Now we come to the more interesting entries.

Nov. 4, 1913 - It is just as impossible to prove or disprove the freedom of the will, as to lift yourself over the fence by your bootstraps. If I feel, or think, my will is free, that is enough for all purposes of my life. If I do not feel or see the necessity that rules me, it is as if it did not exist.

Comment: Of all the things I have ever read or heard about the free will vs. determinism controversy, this strikes me as by far the most sensible! And to think that this should come from one who is *not* a professional philosopher!

July 4, 1859 - A man trying to analyze his own thoughts is like Puss trying to catch her own tail—the greater the effort, the less chance of success. It is only by surprise, by a sudden instantaneous movement of the mind, that we can get an objective view of our own thoughts, as Puss, if she succeeds at all, does by a sudden twist and outreaching before her whole body is in motion. The mind can at best get but a mere glance at its own workings.

There is something very Zen-like in the above passage! The Zen-master, Huang Po, in discussing Mind said: "Begin to reason about it, and you at once fall into error." Also the Zen-master Bankei said: "Trying to cure mind with mind is like trying to wash off blood with blood."

Speaking of Zen, I must make a couple of digressions: An adolescent boy I know was visiting Japan and was smoking a cigarette outside of a Zen temple. The Master came out and gave him a long lecture on why one shouldn't smoke. The boy told me that this was the best-organized set of reasons he had ever heard. When the Zen-master was finished, he reached into his pocket, took out a cigarette, lighted it and started smoking it. The boy said: "How come after all you said, you are smoking?" The Master replied: "Oh, I like it! It tastes good!"

This same boy's brother told me that he once went to a lecture by a famous Indian guru. The guru was close to two hours late. After the lecture, my friend asked one of the guru's young disciples why his master was late. The disciple replied: "He wasn't late! That's typical of your Western way of thinking! He wasn't late; he got there when he did. You thought he was late only because you expected him earlier."

Let us analyze this: True enough; he got there when he did and in *that* sense he was on time. (Every event is on time in that sense.) But also, he *was* late in the sense that he got there later than the time agreed.

As we are on Eastern thought, I read some time ago a review of a Buddhist movie (called, I believe, *Dream Life*), which unfortunately I have never been able to catch. I read that when the Buddhist girl came from India to America and saw all these crazy cult religions going around, she shook her head and said: "When people no longer believe in anything, they are ready to believe *anything!*"

After these digressions, let us go back to John Burroughs' Journal. In a May entry, 1965, he says:

> As necessary as it seems to be in life, much is lost by being wedded to a particular end; and the loafer or saunterer who has nothing at stake, but looks on and contemplates, has the fullest enjoyment.

This passage made a particular personal appeal to me; since I have long loved loafers,

idlers, vagrants, vagabonds, tramps, hoboes—
call them what you will. I believe that they play
a vitally useful role in society.

Book Publishing, Bookselling, and Book Collecting

A great deal of interesting material about Johnson, Boswell and their entire circle can be found in the books of A. Edward Newton. For example, he relates the incident of Johnson's being hailed in the Strand one day by a man who half a century before had been at Pembroke College with him. Johnson did not at first remember his former friend, and was none too pleased to be reminded that they were both "old men now." "We are, sir," said Dr. Johnson, "but do not let us discourage one another." They began to talk over old times and compare notes as to where they stood in the world. Edwards, his friend, had practiced law and had made money, but had spent or given away much of it. "I shall not die rich," said he. "But, sir," said Johnson, "it is better to live rich than to die rich." And now comes Edward's immortal remark: "You are a philosopher, Dr. Johnson. I have tried, too, in my time to be a philosopher, but I don't know how; cheerfulness was always breaking in."

Newton's books are mainly on book collecting—a field that I find fascinating—and are replete with all sorts of interesting historical information. The author is one of the most delightful writers in the field. I am fortunate to possess his books: *The Amenities of Book Collecting* (1918), *A Magnificent Farce* (1912), *The Greatest Book in the World* (1925), *The Book Collecting Game* (1928), *A Tourist In Spite of Himself* (1930), and *End Papers* (1933)—all published by Little, Brown and Company, Boston. Curiously enough I lack one volume of the series—*Dr. Johnson* (1923).

A good friend of his, Dr. A. S. W. Rosenbach, a world famous book collector and dealer of his time, whose book, *Books and Bidders*, I will tell you about later, says the following about Newton:

> A dear friend of mine has been also largely responsible for the modern esteem of old authors. A. Edward Newton, through his popular and appealing books about books, has inspired many to collect them. His *Amenities of Book Collecting* is the bibliophile's Bible; and his enthusiasm for Doctor Johnson is so intense that it is now contagious. Everyone has become infected with it.

In his book, *A Magnificent Farce*, Newton says:

I do not much use any library except my own. I early formed the habit of buying books, and, thank God, I have never lost it. Authors living and dead—dead for the most part—afford me my greatest enjoyment, and it is my pleasure to buy more books than I can read. Who was it who said, "I hold the buying of more books than one can peradventure read, as nothing less than the soul's reaching towards infinity?"

I well sympathize with Newton, though I myself am not a bibliophile, or book collector, in the sense of going out of my way to get first editions or rare books. The books I have bought are all for reading, though I know I will have time to read only a fraction of them. "Why so many books; do I really expect to read them all? Are they just for show?" someone once asked me. Well, As I said, I know that I won't read them all. Are they for show? I wouldn't say exactly that, though I do take great pride in my library and especially of finding passages that will interest my friends and guests. Why do I have as many books as I have? Actually, I don't have all that many (a couple of thousand or so), and my reasons for having them are twofold: First of all, I just love their presence—to use a hackneyed expression, they really are "friends on the shelf." Secondly, I love it when one book sends me to another. It is nice when seeing a reference to another book to actually have the other book within easy reach. And for some reason that I cannot explain—it's almost as if some spirit guided my choice of books—it usually happens that when I come to a reference, the referred book is in my collection.

Although, as I said, I am not one of those who go in for rare books and first editions, I do not share the snobbish attitude of those pedantic scholars who look down on the bibliophile. I greatly respect people like A. Edward Newton and am utterly intrigued reading about their hobby. In the *Amenities of Book Collecting*, Newton says:

> Book collectors are constantly being ridiculed by scholars for the pains they take and the money they spend on first editions of their favorite authors; and it must be that they smart under the criticism, for they are always explaining, and attempting rather foolishly to justify their position. Would it not be better to say, as Leslie Stephen did of Dr. Johnson's rough sayings, that "it is quite useless to defend them to any one who cannot enjoy them without defense"?

A. Edward Newton

In *A Magnificent Farce*, Newton says the following delightful thing about his love of book collecting:

> My philosophy of life is very simple; one doesn't have to study the German philosophers—or any other—to discover that the way to happiness is to get a day's pleasure every day—I am not writing as a preacher—and I know no greater pleasure than taking home a bundle of books which you have deprived yourself of something to buy.

I don't know if Newton was familiar with Skinner's *Mad Folk of The Theatre*, but if he were, he surely would have enjoyed the opening paragraph:

> Unless it be the moment when, after an hour's fruitless whipping of a discouraging stream with every fly in your book from Brown Hackle to Scarlet Ibis, your rod tip bends and your taut line sings to the tug of a two-pound trout, I know no thrill that is comparable to that of the unexpected find of a rare volume in an obscure and shabby book shop. Even that comparison is feeble when the book is one you have long coveted; the thrill lasts longer and its recurrent waves radiate from the stone-splash of your discovery until they are stayed on the shores of

your library shelves, and there they lap in much content.

In the *Amenities* Newton relates the following funny incident:

> Many years ago, in an effort to make conversation on a train—a foolish thing to do—I asked a man what he did with his leisure, and his reply was, "I play cards. I used to read a good deal but I wanted something to occupy my mind, so I took to cards."

Here are some more choice items from A *Magnificent Farce*: He quotes Dr. Johnson as saying:

> Sir, if you want people to read your book, do not give it to them. People value a book most when they buy it.

I'll have to remember that! He quotes Leigh Hunt as saying:

> How satisfactory it is to think of others nobly doing their duty while I am following the bent of my own inclinations.

I love that! You see, I am the opposite of a moralist. I admire Walt Whitman for having written:

I recognize no such thing as duties. What others give as duties, I give as living impulses.

Leigh Hunt's remark also reminds me of a friend of mine who is retired and who told me that it gives him extra pleasure to see other people having to go to work.

Speaking of the diary of Samuel Pepys, Newton says:

> The charm of the *Diary* is its quaint and utter shamelessness, as when its author confesses that he kicked one of his maids and is not sorry for it, but he was sorry that he was seen doing so. Most of us are more like Pepys than we would be willing to confess. We do wrong and carry our heads high, and are ashamed only when we are found out.

I think that's an extremely wise observation! Bertrand Russell once wrote something similar (I can't remember where)—he wrote that our greatest sense of guilt for a crime comes *after* we are found out.

In the chapter "A Sane View of William Blake" Newton quotes two of Blake's verses, which he rightfully says might have come from the pen of Benjamin Franklin:

I was angry with my friend
I told my wrath, my wrath did end.
I was angry with my foe,
I told it not, my wrath did grow.

A truth that's told with bad intent
Beats all the lies you can invent.

I find the second verse particularly apt, and it reminds me of the following: Ayn Rand is hardly one for whom I have much respect, but she once said something I thought very wise: It was during a radio interview and during the question period, one of the audience said: "At the university I come from, the students say that you are very irrational. What do you have to say to that?" She got extremely upset (and I was very sorry for her!) and after defending herself said: "And another thing: Anybody who repeats an insult to me is only insulting me over again!"

How profoundly true! Now back to Newton. In his chapter "Luck," Newton says:

I am a strong believer in luck. I know that Emerson says that luck is the refuge of the shallow, but I don't care much what one philosophy says; I will find you another philosopher who will flatly disagree.

Newton then tells a story he heard of a man who, walking along a country road, noticed a horseshoe lying at his feet, and, picking it up, remarked to himself, "I'm in luck." Then shortly after, he found another, then another and another, until his arms were quite loaded, but then saw some distance in front of him a large wagon full of old, rusty horse-shoes, on its way to the junk heap.

I'm reminded of an ancient Chinese tale I like much better: A farmer had a horse that ran away. All the neighbors came over to console him, but he said: "How do you know this is bad luck?" A few days later, his horse returned with a herd of wild horses. The farmer was now rich. The neighbors came to congratulate him, but he said: "How do you know this is good luck?" A few days later, the farmer's son, riding one of the wild horses was thrown and broke his leg. All the neighbors came over to console him, but he said: "How do you know this is bad luck?" Shortly after, war broke out, and the son, having a broken leg, was spared being drafted into the army.

I call that a profound story! I'm also re-minded of the modern humorous tale of a group of scientists who visited an atomic laboratory, and to their amazement saw a horseshoe and a four-leaf clover over the doorway. They said to the chief scientist: "Surely, you scientists don't believe that sort of thing really works, do you?" The scientist replied: "Of course not, but we understand that they work whether you believe in them or not."

Newton also gave lectures, and when asked his fee, first tells the story of someone when being asked to name his fee for a lecture, replied that he has a three-guinea lecture and a five-guinea lecture and a ten-guinea lecture, but couldn't honestly recommend the three-guinea one. Newton then explains that he himself has only three-guinea lectures in stock, but can't recommend them, especially as he charges a hundred guineas for them.

One learns all sorts of interesting literary odds and ends from Newton's books. For example in *End Papers*, the author tells of a volume of *Poems* by Currer, Ellis and Acton Bell (actually the three Bronte sisters) and that a copy published by Aylott and Jones may be worth five or six hundred pounds (twenty-five hundred or three thousand dollars); whereas the same book with the imprint of Smith, Elder is hardly worth ten pounds. The explanation is that one day Charlotte Bronte found a blank book filled with verses in the handwriting of Emily, and how after much discussion and some correspondence the three sisters—for Anne wrote also—decided upon the publication of a small volume which should contain verses by all of them. But no publisher cared for the venture, until finally Messrs. Aylott and Jones, of London, agreed to publish upon the payment by them of thirty-odd pounds. The girls agreed, and after some delay, the volume appeared. A year later, the publishers reported the sale of just *two* copies. The disappointment of the sisters may be imagined, but they took the blow philosophically and each giving away a copy or two, decided to send the remaining sheets to the trunk makers; but finally having received an offer from Smith, Elder and Company, they transferred the sheets to them, and in due course to the public. Hence it is that a copy of the book with the Aylott and Jones imprint is rare.

Newton was a friend of Sir Henry Fielding Dickens, son of Charles Dickens, who was a judge. He once invited Newton to witness a case involving a coiner (counterfeiter), in which Sir Henry was the presiding judge.

"Are you innocent or guilty?" says Sir Henry.

"Guilty, your Worship."

"I seem to remember you. Have you been in this court before?"

"Yes, your Worship."

"What for?"

"Coining."

"How old are you?"

"Eighty-seven."

Whereupon Sir Henry, turning to a court clerk, says, "Have you this man's record?" It is produced, and Sir Henry glances at it and then, leaning over to Newton says: "God bless my soul, look at this. The man is eighty-seven and has spent forty years in jail. He's entitled to five years at the least, but I can't sentence a man of eighty-seven to five years." Turning to the prisoner: "You're sorry for what you've done, of course?"

"Yes, your Worship."

"And you'd do it again tomorrow, if I let you go?"

"Yes, your Worship."

"I say you'd do it again tomorrow, if I let you go?"

"Yes, your Worship."

"Don't stand there saying 'Yes, your Worship' to me. Is the man deaf?"

"Yes, your Worship."

(Louder) "I say don't stand there saying 'Yes, your Worship' to me. Are you deaf?"

"No, your Worship."

"I'm giving you a very light sentence in consideration of your age. When you come out of prison, where will you go—who will look after you?"

"No, your Worship."

(Louder) "I say who will look after you?"

"My landlady, she will take care of me."

"Well, we'll not let you give her any trouble for twelve months. Twelve months."

"No, your Worship."

"Don't stand there saying 'No, your Worship.' I say twelve months."

The prisoner was taken away, and Sir Henry said to Newton, "They were terribly severe in my father's day in sentencing criminals. At one time this old fellow would have been hung; later he would have been sent to Botany Bay." Upon which Newton suggested that Sir Henry's father had been the father of more reforms in England than all the professed reformers put together and that he would have been very proud to see his own son tempering justice with mercy.

Of course, Newton has much to say in his books about Dickens and about Thackeray. This brings to mind a lovely movie I saw about 40 years ago, whose title I have forgotten, and which was about the Bronte sisters. When one of them (I forget which) was introduced to Thackeray, she said, "You are the *great* Thackeray?" Then Thackeray (who was played by Sidney Greenstreet!) looked down at his corpulent tummy, then back at her and said, "My dear, aren't you being a trifle personal?" (I don't know if this incident was taken from real life or not.) Another cute scene in the movie was when one of the Bronte sisters was walking in the street with Thackeray and a man quickly passed them saying, "Good morning, Master Thackeray." Thackeray replied, "Good morning, Master Dickens." Miss Bronte then asked: "Was that *Charles* Dickens?"

"Why yes, my dear."

"Why didn't you introduce me to him?"

"Now look, my dear; I can't introduce you to every bit of riff-raff in London!"

I very much doubt that this was taken from real life, but I thought it quite funny, nevertheless. And now let me tell you what definitely *is* a true story about Thackeray, and is one of the funniest anecdotes I know. I doubt that it is generally known; I found it in a lovely book by the famous Boston editor, James T. Fields; the book is titled *Yesterdays With Authors* (Houghton, Mifflin and Company, Boston and New York, 1900.) The book, incidentally, has a beautiful blue and gold binding. It is one of my treasures, though I bought it for less than $5. Fields knew Thackeray quite well and relates the following incident:

The most finished and elegant of all *lecturers*, Thackeray, often made a very poor appearance when he attempted to deliver a set speech to a public assembly. He frequently broke down after the first two or three sentences. He prepared what he intended to say with great exactness, and his favorite delusion was that he was about to astonish everybody with a remarkable effort. It never disturbed him that he commonly made a woeful failure when he attempted speech-making, but he sat down with such cool serenity if he found that he could not recall what he wished to say, that his audience could not help joining in and smiling with him when he came to a stand-still.

Once he asked me to travel with him from London to Manchester to hear a great speech he was going to make at the founding of the Free Library Institution in that city. All the way down he was discoursing of certain effects he intended to produce on the Manchester dons by his eloquent appeals to their pockets. This passage was to have great influence with the rich merchants, this one with the clergy, and so on. He said that although Dickens and Bulwer and Sir James Stephen, all eloquent speakers, were to precede him, he intended to beat each of them on this special occasion. He insisted that I should be seated directly in front of him, so that I should have the full force of his magic eloquence.

The occasion was a most brilliant one; tickets had been in demand at unheard-of prices several weeks before the day appointed; the great hall, then opened for the first time to the public, was filled by an audience such as is seldom convened, even in England. The three speeches which came before Thackeray was called upon were admirably suited to the occasion, and most eloquently spoken. Sir John Potter, who presided, then rose, and after some complimentary allusions to the author of *Vanity Fair*, introduced him to the crowd, who welcomed him with ringing plaudits. As he rose, he gave me a half-wink, as if to say: "Now for it; the others have done very well, but I will show 'em a grace beyond the reach of their art."

He began in a clear and charming manner, and was absolutely perfect for three minutes. In the middle of a most earnest and elaborate sentence he suddenly stopped, gave a look of comic despair at the ceiling, crammed both hands into his trousers' pockets, and deliberately sat down. Everybody seemed to understand that it was one of Thackeray's unfinished speeches and there were no signs of surprise or discontent among his audience. He continued to sit on the platform in a perfectly composed manner; and when the meeting was over he said to me, without a sign of discomfiture, "My boy, you have my profoundest sympathy; this day you have accidentally missed hearing one of the finest speeches ever composed for delivery by a great British orator."

William Makepeace Thackeray

Coming back to A. Edward Newton, it is impossible in a short space to do any sort of justice to his first book, *The Amenities of Book Collecting*, though I will say a little. His chapters are titled "Book-Collecting Abroad," "Book Collecting at Home," "Old Catalogues and New Prices," "Association Books and First Editions," "What Might Have Been" (all about Charles Lamb), "James Boswell—His Book," "A Light-Blue Stocking" (all about Johnson's friend Mrs. Thrale), "A Ridiculous Philosopher" (all about William Godwin, the father of Mary Wollstonecraft Shelley), "A Great Victorian" (Anthony Trollope), "Oscar Wilde," and "A Word in Memory" (of Harry Elkins Widener, in whose memory Widener's mother dedicated the famous library in Harvard).

I will say just a little about the final chapter: Widener was an avid book collector and his library was also his bedroom, for he wanted his books about him, where he could play with them at night and where his eye might rest on them the first thing in the morning.

"Are you a book-collector, too?" his grandfather once asked Newton across the dinner table.

Laughingly, Newton said that he thought he was, but not in Harry's class.

To which the old gentleman replied—and his eyes beamed with pride the while—"I am afraid that Harry will impoverish the entire family."

Newton, with his typical sense of humor replied that he should be sorry to hear that, and suggested that Harry and he, if they put their fortunes together, might prevent this calamity.

Later, comes the sad and strange story that when Widener was in London, he bought several books including an excessively rare copy of Bacon's *Essaies*, the edition of 1598. When he dropped in to the bookseller to say goodbye and to give final instructions for the disposition of his purchases, he said: "I think I'll take that little Bacon with me in my pocket, and if I am shipwrecked it will go with me."

How prophetic! He (and the book) went down with the Titanic. His father also went down, but his mother and her maid were saved. He was then age 37.

I have briefly mentioned Dr. A. Rosenbach, whose book, *Books and Bidders* (Little, Brown, and Company, Boston, 1927) I find of equal interest to the works of Newton.

Incidentally, Dr. Rosenbach was not a medical doctor; he was a Ph.D. in English and gave up a university teaching position to become a collector, buyer and seller of books. He was one of the "big" dealers, often paying tens or hundreds of thousands of dollars for a single book.

A funny story is told of a young man browsing through a bookstall in London. A clerk from inside the shop came out exhibiting a cheap dog-eared copy of an autobiography. "How much?" asked the young man cautiously. The clerk replied, "Fourpence." "Fourpence," repeated the other, scandalized. "Who do you think I am—Dr. Rosenbach?"

Uncle Moses once told Rosenbach the story of a man in England, a collector, who heard of some Shakespeare folios in Spain; of how, after months of inquiries and exciting adventures, he at last journeyed to a castle in the Pyrenees. There he found an ancient Spanish grandee leaning forward before a fireplace, feeding the fire with torn bits of paper on which, to his horror, he beheld English printing.

Dr. A. S. W. Rosenbach

He went on to describe how he tore them from the old man's fingers—the remains of a second Shakespeare folio he had sought and found too late.

A happier story is told of how, one afternoon, two young Englishmen were playing archery on an estate near Shrewsbury. Perhaps they didn't have a target, or if they did, they mislaid it. Anyway, they picked up an old book they found somewhere in one of the buildings on the place, and stuck it against the lower branches of a tree to use for a bull's-eye. About to draw his bow, one of them was not quite satisfied with the angle at which they had placed their target, so he walked forward and turned it around. As he did so, some of the pages fell back, and he read the magic name, "Venus." Looking at the volume further, he exclaimed to his companion, "I believe this old thing is similar to that book which sold for 15,100 pounds yesterday!" It soon sold privately for more than 10,000 pounds, or about $50,000. Mr. H. C. Folger of New York, the greatest collector of Shakespeareana was the buyer.

I imagine that the book is now displayed in the world famous Folger Shakespeare Library in

Washington, D. C. Incidentally, I was privileged to know O. B. Hardison, the director of the library for many years. He was kind enough to write endorsements for two of my books.

The above story of the amateur archers illustrates by what strange circumstances rare books can sometimes come to light. Rosenbach's and Newton's books are full of incidents of that nature. For example, Rosenbach tells how the illness of an English barber's wife brought to light a first edition of *The Pilgrim's Progress*: There was a small stack of books which the barber inherited with his shop. One day someone suggested that the books were interesting because they were old, and hence must be valuable (a popular fallacy!). He had heard of a man who once paid two pounds for a book! But the barber said he had plenty to do without chasing about trying to sell old, worn-out books. Then one day, his wife took to her bed and a doctor was hurriedly sent for. While waiting for him, the barber tried to think of some way he might amuse his wife. As he went into the shop, his eyes fell on the books on a low shelf. When the doctor arrived, he found his patient's bed loaded down with books, and she was reading a copy of

The Pilgrim's Progress. The doctor—who knew a little about books—felt there was something unusual about this copy and insisted it should be sent to Sotheby's in London for valuation. The barber reluctantly sent it with a letter of apology, stating that it was probably worthless. Sotheby's was honest enough to reply that it was worth at least $4,000 and that they would put it up for auction. Rosenbach purchased it for about $12,000.

As an example of Rosenbach's shrewdness, he tells how in a sale at the Britwell Court Library in London, he noticed a little book, *Dailey Meditations, Or Quotidian Preparations For and Consideration of Death and Eternity*, by Philip Paine, printed at Cambridge by Marmaduke Johnson in 1668. As it was passed around the room, all the other bookmen looked at it and shook their heads—only a valueless, dull theological work, they thought. But something struck a familiar chord in Rosenbach's memory and suddenly he knew what it was! Marmaduke Johnson it was who had printed in Cambridge, Massachusetts, the first Holy Scriptures issued for the North American Indians—the *Eliot Indian Bible*. Thus, the book was printed in Cambridge, Massachusetts, not Cambridge, England, which made it tremendously rare, because it was the only known copy, hitherto unrecognized, of the first volume of verse printed in North America. You see, all the other bookmen present assumed that it was printed in Cambridge, England, hence had let it go, and Rosenbach bought it for only about $250. After the sale was over, they (including the auctioneer) expressed their surprise that Rosenbach had paid so much for the book, and were thunderstruck when Rosenbach explained what it really was and that he would have been willing to pay up to $50,000 for it.

Speaking of auctions calls to mind a curious incident told to me by an art dealer—an incident that sounds as if it could have been a story written by O'Henry! The dealer purchased a painting of the ex-governor of his state. He realized that the governor somewhere had a son, who would probably pay a fancy price for it. It took him two years to finally locate him, and since the son had no telephone, my friend took the painting directly to his apartment. He rang the bell and the door was opened by a man somewhat inebriated. My friend said: "I have something that I believe will interest you." and unwrapped the painting. "Oh yesh," said the man, "I know that painting; it'sh of my father. I shold it at an auction two yearsh ago."

Alfred Quaritch, a major London bookseller, relates the following incident: One day a stranger called on him with an old book and said that he didn't know its value. Quaritch looked at it and immediately recognized it as the long-lost and valuable edition of a book published in Cambridge, Massachusetts in 1648. Inquiring what the owner wanted for it, the man would not say; he desired Quaritch to make him an offer. After due consideration, Quaritch offered what he considered a fair price—2,500 pounds. The man was thunderstruck (He figured it was worth about 50.) and got quite suspicious and left, saying he would have to think it over. He then shopped around a long time and finally sold it for 5,000 pounds. Quaritch told Rosenbach that it was this experience that cured him forever of making offers on books.

Alfred Quaritch, by the way, inherited the business from Bernard Quaritch—an extremely successful book-seller who died at the turn of the century and who started out with a capital of about ten pounds, saved from the salary of twenty-four shillings a week, which he earned while serving Bohn's bookshop off Convent Garden. If his funds were low, his spirit and ambition were certainly high, for, as the story goes, when Bohn asked him where he was going, he told him frankly that he meant to set up an opposition to his old employer. Bohn laughed and said, "Don't you know that I am the first bookseller in England?" Quaritch replied, "Yes, but I am going to be the first bookseller in Europe," which indeed he did become! I learned this from *The Romance of Bookselling*, by Frank A. Mumby (Little, Brown and Company, Boston, 1911).

In *The Amenities of Book Collecting*, Newton says:

> I knew the elder Quaritch well, and over a cup of tea one winter afternoon years ago, in a cold dingy shop in Piccadilly, he confided in me his fears for his son Alfred. This remarkable old man, who has well been called the Napoleon of booksellers, was certain that Alfred would never be able to carry on the business when he was gone. "He has no interest in books, he is not willing to work hard as he will have to, to maintain the standing I have secured as the

greatest bookseller in the world." Quaritch was very proud, and justly, of his eminence.

How little the old man knew that this son, when the time came, would step into his father's shoes and stretch them. Alfred, when he inherited the business, assumed his father's enthusiasm and shrewdness. He probably surprised himself, as he surprised the world, by adding lustre to the name of Bernard Quaritch, so that, when he died, the newspapers of the English speaking world gave the details of his life and death as matters of general interest.

Bernard Quaritch

I was fascinated to learn from Rosenbach's book about William Tyndale, who felt it his spiritual mission to translate the New Testament from Greek into English—the language of his countrymen. The story is told that one day in a heated dispute with an eminent churchman of England, he was appalled at the other's ignorance of the Scriptures. Then and there, he made the following vow, well-known to theological students ever since: "If God spare my life, ere many years I will cause a boy that driveth his plough to know more of the Scriptures than thou dost."

However, Tyndale could not get any financial backing in England, so he went to Germany. In Hamburg he completed his translation and then went to Cologne, where he hoped to find a printer. It is believed that work on the book was then started, but the Senate of Cologne got suddenly enraged and shocked at the idea of so profane a business going on there, hence an order was sent to the printer to prohibit its continuance, but before it was carried out, Tyndale had fled in panic to Worms, where Martin Luther was then at the height of his popularity. And so the first English translation of the New Testament was published in a small town in Germany!

It was then smuggled into England, where it began to appear. The clergy was furious and Bishop Tunstall, a former friend of Tyndale, had it burned publicly in London. It was burned in other places as well, before crowds of ignorant, superstitious people—indeed, the burnings became a popular pastime. Finally, poor Tyndale was himself burned at the stake.

A funny error occurs in some printings of the 1631 Bible: The word "not" is left out in the seventh commandment, and thus it reads: "Thou shalt commit adultery." Was this what is known as a *Freudian* error? Anyway, only four copies escaped the public executioner, and the printer was fined 300 pounds.

Literary Forgeries, Swindles, Counterswindles, and Magic

My favorite chapter of Rosenbach's book is the one on literary forgeries, which reminds me of a touching incident: A friend of mine, a lady, frequents a certain well-known delicatessen in New York City. One day she saw an elderly lady sneak something into her handbag. My friend told the owner, who smiled and said: "Oh, yes; she's been a very good customer for over twenty-five years, but every now and again she steals a little something." My friend then asked him whether he had ever spoken to her about it. "Oh no," he replied, "that would embarrass her terribly!"

I am also reminded of the joke about a bartender who often, when receiving money from a customer, put some of it into the cash register and some into his own pocket. At one point, he received a dollar bill and put the whole amount into his pocket. At which the boss walked over to him and said, "Jake, since when are we no longer partners?"

Now for the chapter on literary forgeries. Two of my favorite characters of this chapter are William Henry Ireland (whom Rosenbach calls "the greatest fabricator of them all") and Thomas Chatterton. William Henry was the son of an engraver in London, and may well have inherited the facile fingers, which brought him notoriety. The father's greatest desire was to be lucky enough to find an autographed manuscript of Shakespeare. The son's first act of forgery was to skillfully forge one and to present it to his father as genuine, making up a story that he had met a gentleman of fortune, whose name he had sworn not to tell, who shared his love of things antique. The gentleman then invited him to his house and allowed him to rummage through some old papers tied together in bundles. Then, to their mutual joy, he discovered an old paper that definitely established the friend's right to a certain property, which had been the subject of long litigation. In gratitude, the friend after swearing him to secrecy, presented him with as many of his ancient manuscripts as he wished to have.

This was his story, and the father believed it and was delighted and told it to his friends, who also believed it. Intoxicated with his success, the son grew more and more daring and then, in

Rosenbach's words: "When less than eighteen years, pulled the leg of almost the entire literary world with his 'discovery' of many Shakespearean manuscripts." In fact, Boswell called at Ireland's home one day and inspected the manuscripts. He then knelt down before them and enthusiastically kissed the paper here and there as he thanked God for letting him live to see them.

Most remarkable of all, Ireland wrote a pretended play of Shakespeare, entitled *Vortigern and Rowena*, which fooled the literary community to the point that the play was actually produced by Sheridan with two of the foremost players of the day, John Philip Kemble and Dora Jordan, appearing in the leading roles. (By God, to be able to fabricate a Shakespeare play and successfully so, even if for only a short time, takes what I call *talent*! If only historical delights like this were taught in schools, I think we would have far more history enthusiasts.)

Unfortunately, it was this play that finally undid him, and Ireland made a full public confession. The amazing thing is that after his misdeeds were discovered, collectors and curio seekers everywhere wanted to own specimens of his interesting fraudulent papers, and so Ireland was then kept busy from morning till night making forgeries of his forgeries and selling them as original forgeries! Now, that's what I call irrepressible, incorrigible persistence!

In his public confession, Ireland spoke of being influenced by reading the career of the earlier youthful forger Thomas Chatterton who, if anything, is even more interesting

Chatterton began writing when he was sixteen and according to many, wrote some of the finest poetry in the history of the eighteenth-century literature. But the amazing thing is that instead of publishing under his own name, he claimed that they were all written by the fifteenth century monk, Thomas Rowley. He claimed that his father had found them years earlier in an ancient chest belonging to the Church of St. Mary Redcliffe at Bristol.

At first, this story was believed and critics praised the great beauty of the poems. But then suspicions grew and Chatterton was charged with having written these poems using a certain dictionary from which he chose Anglo-Saxon words in order to create an antique atmosphere and flavor. Among his worse critics were

Horace Walpole and his two poet friends, Mason and Gray. Instead of praising Chatterton for the magnificence of the poems, all they could harp on was the fact that they were forgeries. Poor Chatterton could not stand the goading of Walpole and his acolytes and committed suicide at the age of eighteen! Rosenbach, whose sympathies were clearly with Chatterton (and so are mine!) says: "A few of the inspired lines of Chatterton's poems are worth all the famous letters Walpole so elegantly wrote for a large public, including himself.

Ah, yes, forgeries and swindles; why do they intrigue me so? Could it be due to my years spent as a magician? Probably! All magic is a swindle, in a sense; and now let me tell you of what I would call a *counterswindle* (I believe I've just coined a new word.) As most of you know, Harry Houdini could escape from just about any locked cell in a matter of minutes, but he was once cleverly "counterswindled" by a British police officer: Instead of getting out of his cell in minutes, it took him hours. All his usual tricks for opening locks failed. Hours, later, he suddenly guessed the truth: The police officer had only *pretended* to lock the door, which had been open all that time! Now, that's what I call a brilliant counterswindle!

Speaking of Houdini, I must tell you that Sir Conan Doyle, in his days when he became fanatically involved with spiritualism, insisted that the way Houdini escaped from locked trunks was to de-materialize and exit through the keyhole! Nothing that Houdini could tell him would convince him that this was not so. Doyle was incredibly stubborn in his later years: There was one British mind-reading team—husband and wife—and after one performance, Doyle went backstage to congratulate them on their "psychic powers." The husband said: "I'm sorry to disappoint you, but we don't have psychic powers. We use signals." Doyle left saying: "You must have psychic powers, whether you realize it or not."

A funny story: Sir Conan and Lady Doyle once took Houdini to a medium, who they said would contact Houdini's deceased mother. The medium went into a deep trance and words came pouring out. The Doyles were quite impressed, but Houdini was laughing the whole time. After the séance, on the way out, Doyle asked Houdini why he was laughing. Houdini replied: "If that had been my mother, the only language she could have spoken is Yiddish. She didn't know a word of English.

Next, I must tell you a very moving story about Harry and Beatrice Houdini: As many of you know, Houdini was a lifelong exposer of the fraudulent tricks used by mediums. Nevertheless, he wanted to be open-minded, and so he told his wife Beatrice that if he should go before her, if there was any possibility of doing so, he would contact her during the first six months after his death. Shortly after, he died. The Christmas after, I bought a copy of the British magic magazine, *The Sphinx*, and on the back cover, in large letters was a Christmas Message from Mrs. Houdini:

DEAR HARRY,
YOU WERE RIGHT AS USUAL. YOU DIDN'T COME BACK.

Speaking of magic, let me tell you my favorite trick of all time! It was performed by Sam Lloyd, who was one of the greatest inventors of puzzles the world has ever known, and was also an excellent magician. His trick, which I am about to describe, even fooled magicians. It was done aboard a ship. He blindfolded his little boy and then turned him so that his back was to the audience. Then one of the spectators (not a confederate!) took a perfectly normal deck of cards supplied by the ship's crew, shuffled them thoroughly and showed the faces one by one to Sam Lloyd, who said not a word, nor tapped his foot, nor made any sound whatsoever, yet as each card was shown to Sam, the little boy would correctly name it! Radios were not yet invented; in fact no electrical signal of any kind could have been used. As I said, it fooled even magicians. How was it done? I'll let you try to guess for a while and I'll tell you later!

Speaking of swindles, some very neat ones have been described by Edgar Allan Poe (one of my favorite authors), only he calls them "diddles," not "swindles," and his essay on this profound subject is titled "Diddling"—more completely, "Diddling, considered as one of the exact sciences." He believes that the definition of man as a featherless biped should be replaced by: "Man is the one and only creature who diddles." One of Poe's cutest diddles concerns a man who goes into a very large shop, pretends to be the proprietor and accepts money for a purchase, promising to have it delivered the next day.

My favorite of all swindles is known as the *ten-dollar bar swindle*, and was played around the turn of the century. It has to be done at a large bar in which there are two cash registers. The magician entertains the customers near one of them and then announces that he will do the greatest trick of the evening! He asks the bartender to take a ten-dollar bill from the cash register and pencil his name on it. He then takes the bill from the bartender, puts it into an envelope, which he then seals. Now, the envelope has a slit in the back, and so the magician removes the bill through the slit, palms it and hands it to a confederate. (Nobody knows he has a confederate!) Then he says: "Now I will burn the bill and the envelope." While he is making preparations for the burning, the confederate goes to the other cash register, where there is another bartender, orders a drink for a dollar, gives the ten dollar bill and gets nine dollars change. Then the magician sets fire to the envelope, and after it has completely burned says: "And now for my miracle! I shall make the bill reappear wholly restored. You will find it in that other cash register over there!" A scout is sent to the other register, and sure enough, there is found the bill with the bartender's name on it. Everyone applauds!

I also like subtle swindles in advertising, such as the advertisement that once came out for weight reducing: "Guaranteed to lose up to five pounds a week."

I recently saw a cute cartoon in the New Yorker in which a salesman was pointing to an article and said, "This costs less than those selling for twice as much!"

The following strikes me as more an error than a deception: One company advertised: "No detail is small enough to be overlooked." (In other words, all details are sufficiently large to be overlooked.) The funny thing about this is that it seems right at first. It reminds me of that baffler: "I couldn't fail to disagree with you less!"

I am reminded of a very logical child of six who was once at a banquet. At one point the hostess asked him: "Would you like some more chicken?" The little boy said: "No." His mother, who was sitting next to him reprimandingly said: "No, *what*, dear?" He replied: "No chicken."

A joking swindle I once played on one of my graduate students who was writing his Ph.D. thesis with me: In a letter I wrote him, I said: "And if you have any questions, don't hesitate to call me collect and reverse the charges."

Now, I will tell you how Sam Lloyd did his trick: The child never said a word; Sam Lloyd was a ventriloquist! Now, can you think of any cleverer swindle than that? I told you that even magicians were fooled (It was a totally new and original idea!) and the funny thing is that one old man said to Sam Lloyd: "You shouldn't strain the boy's mind that much; it's not good for him!"

And now we turn to the particularly delightful topics of leisure, idleness, and quietude!

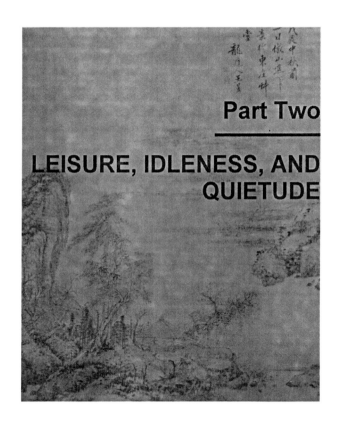

Part Two

LEISURE, IDLENESS, AND QUIETUDE

Personal Observations and Views

The psychiatrists—at least the psychoanalytically oriented ones—tell us that we all have our own idealized image of ourselves. Some of these idealized images are rather curious: I recall Karen Horney somewhere telling us of one man whose idealized image included, among other things, turning at night into a werewolf. Also Chuangtse writes:

> The clansman T'ai, now—he lay down peaceful
> and easy;
> he woke up wide-eyed and blank.
> Sometimes he thought he was a horse;
> sometimes he thought he was a cow.
> His understanding was truly perfect.

Well now, I am also human; hence I too have an idealized image. My idealized image—or perhaps I should say "secret ambition"—is to be known as a philosopher of leisure, idleness and quietude. And if the revolution should ever come, I should like to be made commissar of leisure, idleness, laziness, escapism, elitism, ivory towerism, quietism and solitude.

The funny thing is that since I got interested in this whole subject and started engaging in "research" on it (sic!), I have never been so busy in my whole life; I hardly have an idle moment to myself! As one astute friend who knows me well said: "At least he has found something to keep him busy."

Now I shall write for you a nice long, leisurely and rambling essay on all these matters, in which we will take an unhurried look at the thoughts of several writers. Like Chuangtse, I wish to put my ideas into "indefinite cup-like words, ascribing them to others for authority."

We first turn to Bertrand Russell. In his delightful essay, "In Praise of Idleness." He in effect stated that although he was brought up with the view that one should be industrious, and his conscience has accordingly kept him busy, his *views* have completely changed. In his present view, far too much work is done in the world, and that great harm is done by preaching that work is virtuous. What *should* be preached, he maintains, is the very opposite. He hoped that after reading his essay, the YMCA would start a campaign to induce young men to do nothing.

Of course a lot of this was tongue in cheek, but I still agree with a lot of his ideas. My own attitude towards work is just about the diametric opposite of that of the so-called "work ethic." To me, the necessity to work is one of the greatest evils in life. And when I say "necessity," I refer only to economic necessity, not to one's inner artistic intellectual or spiritual necessity. That is to say, I find it a tragic evil— for which no one can be blamed—that we have to work in order to eat. And I am certainly not advocating shirking that work which is necessary, but am only against this deplorable tendency to regard this necessity as somehow "desirable." In short, I feel that necessary work should be bravely tolerated as a necessary evil, and unnecessary work should be summarily abolished as an unnecessary evil. The one thing I cannot stand is this horrible maxim "Work is good for us."

There are indeed some compulsive workers for whom work is about the only escape from unbearable psychological problems. And for some, work is an escape from boredom. Indeed, I was surprised recently when I asked a new woman working at a food market, "How do you like your job?" She replied: "Very much. It gives me something to do."

Just what is work? Russell provides this delightful answer: Work is of two types—one is moving matter about, and the other is ordering other people to do so. The first kind is unpleasant and poorly paid, whereas the second is pleasant and highly paid.

In a less charming, but more serious vein, I should like to tell you just what I mean by "work" as an evil. To me, work is of the following two kinds: The first is that work which one has to do in order to live, and which one would not do otherwise; and the second is that work which one would do even if there were no remuneration whatsoever. For example, if I asked a teacher: "If you were economically independent, would you continue to teach?" If he answered "No," then he would be working in the first sense; if he said, "Yes," then he would be working in the second sense. Obviously, it is only work in the first sense that I regard as tragic; I hardly think this of the second! Indeed, work in the second sense is obviously one of the greatest joys in one's life. But work in this sense can come remarkably close in spirit to that of leisure! I have the highest regards for all of those who are extremely productive, yet who have felt that their whole lifelong "work" was essentially one grand leisurely hobby! This, of course, is the quintessence of the Taoist spirit. And we do not have to go as far as the Far East to find this spirit; our own culture affords some gorgeous examples. One such is the eighteenth century English poet and scholar, Thomas Gray—at least, according to the following fascinating biographical sketch by David Ferry in *British Literature*, 3rd ed. (D. C. Heath, 1974) that begins thus:

> As Joseph Wood Crutch says, Gray's life was "a series of retirements from what is commonly called living," the withdrawn and uncompetitive life of a sequestered scholar…He was thought by at least one admirer to be "the most learned man in Europe," and indeed the extent of his learning was astonishing, ranging from ornithology, botany, other sorts of natural history, to current politics, diplomacy, economics, history to architecture, to painting, music, the theatre, to the northern literatures and mythologies, and of course the classics. William Hazlitt says of him: "He had nothing to do but read and to think, and to tell his friends what he read and thought. His life was a luxurious thoughtful dream." The

luxuriousness of the dream needn't imply indolence; the detail and scrupulosity of his knowledge is as impressive as his range. But Hazlitt's word "dream" does imply the special relation of Gray's intellectual life to his temperament. He is an instance of a familiar eighteenth century type, often described as the scholar-poet-amateur, a man whose interests are all, as it were, hobbies—and pursued with an alert intelligence that commands respect, but hobbies nevertheless. Even his poetry, it might be said, was a hobby for him, though of the most serious kind. At any rate, he was accustomed to speak of it as if this were so. He was for a time the most celebrated living poet in England, yet he seems to have been more or less indifferent to his fame and there is small reason to think that his indifference was pretended. It seems rather to have been another aspect of his self-sequestration.

Is not this sketch an utterly Taostic dream? I can imagine some Puritanical critic reading this, frowning and saying, "This is completely elitist!" But I shall ignore such critics. Apart from the emphasis of regarding one's main activity as a "leisurely hobby" (which is one of my favorite themes in life) I was particularly struck by the phrase "familiar eighteenth century type, the scholar-poet-amateur whose interest are all, as it were, hobbies." What struck me is the remarkable similarity of this to the views of many of the classical Chinese literati. There appears to be a fascinating temperamental affinity between much Chinese and eighteenth century British thought.

Of course, I think that we should make a definite distinction between idleness and leisure. In fact, there is an important difference between idleness and leisure. And of the two, I think, leisure is even better. But this does not mean that idleness is all that bad! One marvelous thing about the Taoists is that they do not regard the aimless idle life as necessarily undesirable; they believe it can have a certain beauty all its own, which they compare with that of wild flowers growing in a canyon never beheld by human eyes. However, there seems to be a lingering tendency of many to insist that the cult of leisure and idleness is for just the wealthy class.

Late Nineteenth and Early Twentieth Century Western Views

I am particularly fond of relatively obscure authors who have fallen out of vogue, and who are accordingly not nearly as widely known as they should be. I shall introduce you to two such authors now. The first of these is the Philadelphian essayist, Agnes Repplier. It is unbelievable how few people these days have ever heard of her! I first came across a discussion of her in A. Edward Newton's book, *End Papers*. I have just about all of Agnes Repplier's books (around 20 volumes). The one we shall now look at is called *Essays in Idleness* (*Essays in Idleness*, Houghton Mifflin & Co., Boston and New York, 1894). And the particular essay I wish to consider is called "Leisure." In it, she says the following interesting and delightful things about Samuel Johnson:

> Dr. Johnson, too, had scant sympathy with insistent and arrogant industry. He could work hard enough when circumstances demanded it; but he "always felt an inclination to do nothing," and not infrequently gratified his desires. "No

man, sir, is obliged to do as much as he can. A man should have part of his life to himself." was the good doctor's soundly heterodox view, advanced upon many occasions. He hated to hear people boast of their assiduity, and nipped such vain pretensions in the bud with frosty scorn. When he and Boswell journeyed together in the Harwich stage-coach, a "fat, elderly gentlewoman," who had been talking freely of her own affairs, wound up saying that she never permitted any of her children to be for a moment idle. "I wish, Madam," said Dr. Johnson testily "that you would educate me too, for I have been an idle fellow all my life." "I am sure, Sir," protested the woman with dismayed politeness, "you have not been idle." "Madam," was the retort, "it is true! And that gentleman there"—pointing to poor young Boswell—"has been idle also. He was idle in Edinburgh. His father sent him to Glasgow, where he continued to be idle. He came to London, where he has been very idle. And now he is going to Utrecht, where he will be as idle as ever."

That there was a background of truth in these spirited assertions, we have every reason to be grateful. Dr. Johnson's value today does not depend on the number of essays, or reviews, or dedications he wrote in a year—some years he wrote nothing—but on his own study and splendid personality, "the real primate, the soul's teacher of all England," says Carlyle, "a great embodiment of uncompromising goodness and sense. Every generation needs such a man, not to compile dictionaries, but to preserve the balance of sanity, and few generations are blest enough to possess him. As for James Boswell, he might have toiled in the law courts until he was gray without benefiting or amusing anybody. It was in the nights he spent drinking port wine at the Mitre, and in the days he spent trotting, like a terrier, at his master's heel, that the seed was sown, which was to give the world a masterpiece of literature, the most delightful biography that has ever enriched mankind. *It is to leisure that we owe the **Life of Johnson**, and a heavy debt we must, in all integrity acknowledge it to be.*" (Italics mine.)

Miss Repplier begins her essay with some lovely remarks about Voltaire:

A visitor strolling through the noble woods of Ferney complimented Voltaire on the splendid growth of his trees. "Ay," replied the great wit, half in scorn and half, perhaps, in envy, "they have nothing else to do." and walked on, deigning no further word of approbation…How is it that, while Dr. Johnson's sledge-hammer repartees sound like the sonorous echoes of a past age, Voltaire's remarks always appear to have been spoken the day before yesterday.

Other passages of the essay:

"The Gospel of Work"—that is the phrase woven insistently into every homily, every appeal made to the conscience or intelligence of a people who are now straining their youthful energy to its utmost speed. "Blessed be Drudgery"—that is the text deliberately chosen for a discourse which has enjoyed such amazing popularity that sixty thousand printed copies have been found all inadequate to supply the ravenous demand.

Apropos of this, I recall, about twenty-five years ago in Chicago, I passed a church outside of which was printed the title of the Sunday sermon: "To labor is to pray." It gave me the shudders!

To return to the essay:

"A whole lifetime of horrid industry,"— to quote Mr. Bagehot's uninspired words—this is the prize dangled alluringly before our tired eyes…" Our virtues would be proud if our faults whipped them not…" It is the peon of self-glorification that wells up perpetually from press to pulpit.

Later on, she makes some nice remarks about Montaigne:

And what of the leisure of Montaigne, who, taking his life in his two hands, disposed of it as he thought fit, with no restless self-accusations on the score of indolence. In the world and of the world, yet always able to meet and greet the happy solitude of Gascony, *toiling with no thought of toil*, but rather "to entertain my spirit as it best pleased," this man wrought out of time a coin which passes current over the reading world. (Italics mine).

The phrase "toiling with no thought of toil" particularly struck me. I have long maintained that the real difference between leisure and so-called "work" is entirely one of attitude; it is not the amount of activity that counts, but purely the spirit in which it is undertaken. There is a beautiful Chinese saying: "The Sage never tries, never strives, never makes an effort. Yet everyone around comments on how hard he is working." (This, by the way, is a perfect application of the principle known as Wu Wei).

To return to the essay, Miss Repplier then speaks of Horace:

...And what of Horace, who enjoyed an industrious idleness, the bare description of which sets our hearts aching with desire! "The picture which Horace draws of himself in his country home," says an envious English critic, "affords us a delightful glimpse of such literary leisure as is only possible in the golden days of good Haroun-Al-Rashid. Horace goes to bed and gets up when he likes; there is no one to drag him down to the law courts the first thing in the morning, to remind him of an important engagement with his brother scribes, to solicit his interest in Maecenas, or to tease him about public affairs and the latest news from abroad. He can bury himself in his Greek authors, or ramble through the woody glens which lie at the foot of Mount Ustica, without a thought of business or a feeling that he ought to be otherwise engaged.

Apropos of Horace's "going to bed and getting up when he likes," I have all my life maintained that one of the greatest—and unfortunately inadequately recognized—evils of our civilization is that human beings have to get up with an alarm clock! I cannot think of anything more profoundly barbarous! And I have always been amazed at the lack of protest and indignation on this score. I recall once voicing these views to a sociologist, who became extremely agitated, and who characterized my attitude as "effete" and "decadent." To me, it is simple common sense. I recall, about thirty years ago, reading somewhere about a sizable group of centigenarians living either in Russia or Siberia

(I forget which). They were interviewed by a panel of doctors who were trying to ascertain what life habits might be responsible for their remarkable longevity. The one response that was unanimous was that all of them had, their whole lives long, "always slept themselves out, and only got up after they had felt fully rested."

Agnes Repplier, Charles G. Osgood (standing), and Mr. and Mrs. Newton in the library at "Oak Knoll."

The following passages of Miss Repplier's should be of particular interest to those interested in education:

...It can hardly be denied that the lack of scholarship—of classical scholarship especially—at our universities is due primarily to the labor-worship which is the prevalent superstition of our day, and which, like all superstitions, has gradually degraded its god into an idol, and lost sight of the higher powers and attributes beyond. The student who is pleased to think a knowledge of German "more useful" that a knowledge of Greek; the parent who deliberately declares that his boys have "no time to waste" over Homer; the man who closes the doors of his mind to everything that does not bear directly on mathematics, or chemistry, or engineering, or whatever he calls "work;" all these plead in excuse the exigencies of life, the absolute and imperative necessity of labor.

...The notion that it is worthwhile to learn a thing only if you intend to impart it to others is widespread and exceedingly popular. I have myself heard an excellent and anxious aunt say to her young niece, then working hard at college, "But, my dear, why do you give so much of your time to Greek? You don't expect to teach it, do you?"—as if there were no other use to be gained, no other pleasure to be won from that noble language, in which lies hidden the hoarded treasure of centuries. To study Greek in order to read and enjoy it, and thereby make life better worth the living, is a possibility that seldom enters the practical modern mind.

About Walter Scott, Miss Repplier says:

Mr. Shortreed said truly of Sir Walter Scott that he was "making himself in the busy, idle pleasures of his youth;" in those long rambles by hill and dale those whimsical adventures in farmhouses, those merry, purposeless journeys in which the eager lad tasted the flavor of life. At home such unauthorized amusements were regarded with emphatic disapprobation. "I greatly doubt, sir," said his father to him one day, "that you were born for nae better than a gangrel scrape-gut!"…In his later years Sir Walter recognized keenly that his wasted school hours entailed on him a lasting loss, a loss he was determined his sons should never know. It is to be forever regretted that "the most Homeric of modern men could not read Homer." But every day he stole from the town to give to the country, every hour he stole from law to give to literature, every minute he stole from work to give to pleasure, counted in the end as gain. It is in his pleasures that a man really lives; it is from his leisure that he constructs the true fabric of self.

About Charles Lamb, Miss Repplier says:

Charles Lamb has recorded distinctly his veneration for the old-fashioned school-master who taught his Greek and Latin in leisurely fashion day after day, with no thought wasted upon more superficial or practical acquirements, and who "came to his task as a sport."...

...Perhaps Charles Lamb's fellow clerks thought that because his days were spent at a desk in the East India House, his life was spent there too. His life was far remote from that routine of labor; built up of golden moments of respite, enriched with joys, chastened by sorrows, vivified by impulses that had no filiation with his daily toil. "For the time that a man may call his own," he wrote to Wordsworth, "that is his life." The Lamb who worked in the India House, and who had "no skill in figures," has passed away, and is today but a shadow and a name. The Lamb of the "Essays" and the "Letters" lives for us now, and adds each year his generous share to the innocent gayety of the world. This is the Lamb who said, "Riches are chiefly good because they give us time," and who sighed for a little son that he might christen him Nothing-to-do, and permit him to do nothing.

The concept of "quietude" is even deeper, more profound, than that of idleness or leisure. I think one of the greatest philosophers of quietude I have found is Hamilton Wright Mabie. To my amazement, he is also virtually unknown! I know one teacher of literature at a university who just gave a course in Emerson, Whitman and Thoreau, and who never even heard of Mabie! I am particularly surprised, since Mabie impresses me as equal to the other three. Perhaps I was partial, since Mabie is, most of the time, so extremely Taoistic. (I do not know that Mabie knew anything about Taoistic writings; nevertheless, his temperament is a very Taoistic one). I think a good Ph. D. topic for a graduate student in literature might be: "Taoism in the writings of Hamilton Wright Mabie." I hope someone will take this up!

My favorite of Mabie's books is probably *Essays in Nature and Culture* (Dodd, Mead & Co., 1901).

Three of the essays of this collection are entitled "Repose," "Solitude and Silence" and "Unhasting, Unresting." I will begin with "Repose."

The process of growth, with the evidence of which the world overflows, is as mysterious as the vital principle behind it. We can lay our hands on all sides on its results; but we never actually see it. We cannot accurately mark its stages, nor can we exactly measure it by time duration; we can say of it, however, that it is the unfolding of that which lies in the germ by the appropriation of those elements that assimilate with it. There is one quality that everywhere characterizes it—the quality of repose. The living thing that grows, whatever its form, surrenders itself entirely to the process. It does not vacillate between different aims; it is in no uncertainty as to its type; it makes no experiments in the choice of the elements upon which it is to draw sustenance. By the law under which it lives it selects the things which it needs, and opens itself to their reception. It is always expanding, and it is always in repose; for repose implies neither sluggishness nor inactivity; it means quietness and calmness at the center of activity. Emerson long ago noted, as others had noted before him, that the Greek heroes, no matter how strenuously engaged, are always in repose. In this attitude, it need hardly be said, these typical figures are in harmony with the spirit of Greek art; an art which was close to Nature, and which is still, in many of its aspects, the most complete expression and interpretation of Nature...

...There is nothing more impressive as an exhibition of power than the expansion of a great tree, and its power of resisting the storms and winds; but that process is soundless. Eternal quiet seems to brood in the shadow of this miracle of strength and silence. The depth and range of the growth of the human spirit are conditioned on a kindred repose…

I wish to interrupt for a moment to tell you the following incident: I gave this essay to a mathematician friend of mine who was visiting me. At one point of reading the essay (at about the point I have just stopped) he turned to me with astonishment and said, "This sounds Chinese!" It sure does sound Chinese! More specifically, it sounds most Taoistic, which it is. I particularly love Mabie's comparison of the growth of the human spirit to the silent growth of a tree. I have always admired most those creative workers whose work grows inconspicuously but after a while amazes everyone. This is an application of the important Taoist concept "Wu Wei" or "unforced action." Chuangtse said: "The sage never strives, never tries, never makes and effort. Yet everyone around says he is working so hard!"

Now, some passages from "Solitude and Silence":

The sense of freedom which comes when one goes into the deep woods is something more than the satisfaction of a physical need; it is the satisfaction of a spiritual need—the need of isolation, detachment, solitude. To the mind fatigued by constant and rapid adjustments to different subjects and to diverse tasks, the quiet and seclusion of the woods are like a healing balm. The pleasure they bring with them is so keen and so real that it is almost sensuous. One feels as if he had found himself after a touch of delirium. The silence is sedative and the solitude a tonic; relaxation and reinvigoration are both at hand.

The instinct which impels us to get away from our fellows is as normal as that which constantly draws us to them; we cannot really live without them; we cannot really live with them! Here, as elsewhere, the highest growth involves the harmonization of two apparently opposing human conditions—the condition of isolation and that of association...

...No man can give the highest impulses and thoughts to his fellows until he is, in a certain sense, independent of them; the visions of the prophet come in the desert or on the lonely summit of the hill. His duty is to his fellows, but much of the truth of which he is the mouthpiece is revealed to him when he is wrapped about with silence and solitude.

Now a little bit from Mabie's essay "Unhasting, Unresting":

...Nature can produce a finished form in an hour, or she can spend a thousand years in the performance of a single task; in both cases she is equally exact, thorough, and adequate in selection of material and use of instruments; and she is also equally easeful, leisurely, and unhasting. She never rests and she never hastens; she is always at her task and she is always at her ease.

This is reminiscent of Laotse's "The Tao does not *do* anything, yet through it, all things get done."

To continue:

...And in no aspect of her life is Nature more suggestive than in this fruitful repose, this energetic quietness, this masterful ease. We fret and worry and strain; we toil and groan and fall; she goes calmly on with her play of forces and tools, and accomplishes ends which not only lie beyond our strength, but beyond the limits our comprehension...

...It is significant that the higher and more enduring the form of work is, the closer the parallelism between the method of Nature and the method of man.

Two comments: I think the phrase "energetic quietness" is really a remarkable English equivalent of "Wu Wei." This surely is one meaning of the Chinese term, and one that I have never seen given by any translator. The second thing which I would like to point out is Mabie's thoroughly Taoistic attitude regarding human creativity—at its best—as similar to the workings of Nature itself; indeed, in several other essays, Mabie appears to have the generally Eastern attitude of regarding Art itself as arising out of Nature.

In Mabie's book, *My Study Fire* (Dodd, Mead & Co., 1897), he has two relevant essays: "The Bliss of Solitude" and "A Word for Idleness." He begins the latter thus:

> The study fire is sometimes so potent a solicitation to reverie that I ask myself whether it be not a subtle kind of temptation. Even when a man has cleared himself of the cant of the day, as Carlyle would put it, and delivered himself of the American illusion that every hour not devoted to "doing something" is an hour wasted, the inherited instinct is still strong enough to make an appeal to conscience. Those active, aggressive words, "doing" and "getting," have so long usurped the greater part of the space in our vocabulary that we use the words being and growing with a little uncertainty; most of us are not entirely at ease with them yet.

How true, these last words! Later on, Mabie ways:

...Busy people are often painfully barren and uninteresting. Their activity expends itself in small mechanical ways, which add nothing to the sum of human knowledge or happiness. On the other hand, people who are apparently idle, who seem to be detached from the working world, are often the most fruitful. Our standard of work and idleness are in sad need of revision—a revision which shall substitute character for mere activity, and measure work and achievement by the depth and richness of nature disclosed.

Mabie ends the essay with the following sublime words:

...The deepest life is as silent as the soil out of which the glory of summer burst; all noble activities issue from it, and no great work is ever done save by those who have lived in the repose which precedes creation.

Ancient Greek and Roman Views

Now let us turn to the Greeks and Romans. The following is from Plato's *Thaetatus* (*The Dialogues of Plato*, B. Jowett tr., Vol.IV, Oxford University Press, 1892):

Socrates - Here arises a new question, Theodorus, which threatens to be more serious than the last.

Theodorus - Well, Socrates, we have plenty of leisure.

Socrates - That is true, and your remark recalls to my mind an observation which I have often made, that those who have passed their days in the pursuit of philosophy are ridiculously at fault when they have to appear and speak in court. How natural is this?

Theodorus - What do you mean?

Socrates- I mean to say, that those who have trained in philosophy and liberal pursuits are as unlike those who from their youth upwards have been knocking about in the courts and such places, as a freeman is in breeding unlike a slave.

Theodorus - In what is the difference seen?

Socrates - In the leisure spoken of by you, which a freeman can always command: he can talk out in peace, and like ourselves, he wanders at will from one subject to another, and from a second to a third—if the fancy takes him, he begins again, as we are doing now, caring not whether his words are many or few; his only aim is to attain the truth. But the lawyer is always in a hurry; there is the water of the *clepsydra* driving him on, and not allowing him to expatiate at will; and there is his adversary standing over him, enforcing his rights, the indictment, which in their phraseology is termed the affidavit, is recited at the time; and from this he must not deviate. He is a servant, and is continually disputing about a fellow-servant before his master, who is seated, and has the cause in his hands; the trial is never about some indifferent matter, but always concerns himself; and often the race is for his life. The consequence has been, that he has become keen and shrewd; he has learned how to flatter his master in word and indulge him in deed; but his soul is small and unrighteous. He has been a slave from his youth...Will you have the comparison picture of the philosopher, or shall we return to the argument?

In Sebastian de Grazia's interesting book, *Of Time, Work, and Leisure*, (Doubleday and Co.,

Garden City, New York, 1964) he has four marvelous sentences which are about as Taoistic or Buddhistic as anything I have ever seen!

> The man in contemplation is a free man. He needs nothing. Therefore nothing determines or distorts his thought. He does whatever he loves to do, and what he does is done for its own sake.

I think a whole volume of commentary could be written on those four sentences! Aristotle says elsewhere (in the *Metaphysics*):

> At first he who invented any art whatever that went beyond the common perceptions was naturally admired by men, not only because there was something useful in the inventions, but because he was thought wise and superior to the rest. But as more arts were invented, and some were directed to the necessities of life, others to recreation, the inventors of the latter were naturally always regarded as wiser than the inventors of the former, because their branches of knowledge did not aim at utility. Hence when all such inventions were already established, the sciences which do not aim at giving pleasure or at the necessities of life were discovered, and first in the places where men began to have leisure. This is why the mathematical arts were founded in Egypt; for there the priestly caste was allowed to be at leisure.

The Emperor Julian solemnly declared that whoever tries to persuade us that the philosophical life—meaning the life of leisure and contemplation—is not superior to everything else, is trying to cheat us.

Well said, Emperor Julian. Well said! I salute you two thousand and odd years back in the past!

De Grazia concludes his discussion of Seneca with this very moving remark:

> What one should aim for is to be able to say, as Seneca expresses in a letter, "I am free, Lucillius, free, and wherever I am, I am myself."

CHINESE VIEWS

Now we shall turn to the Chinese. I have many
Chinese poetry books in my library and, in fact,
I love Chinese poetry so much that I have made
my own versions of my favorite Chinese poems.
The following poem is charmingly relevant and
is my version of Chuangtse's *The Active Life*.

If an expert has no problems to worry over,
  he is not happy.
If a philosopher's words are not attacked,
  he pines away.
If critics have no one to malign,
  they are unhappy.
Such men are enmeshed
  in the world of illusion.
The strong man looks for
  heavy weights to lift.
The brave man looks for
  disasters in which he can show his bravery.
The swordsman looks for
  battles in which he can brandish his sword.
Men in their advanced years
  seek a dignified retirement
  in which they may appear profound.
The man of law seeks difficult cases
  in which he can show off his skill.
The musician likes gatherings
  where he can display his talent.

The moralist is always looking
  to show his virtue.
How would the gardener survive
  if there were no weeds to cut?
How would business survive
  without a market of dupes?
How would labor survive if there
  were no unnecessary objects to be made?
Where would the crowds be
  if they had no pretext for getting together
  and making lots of noise?
Be active! Get things done!
Make money! Make changes!
Or you will die of frustration!
Those who are caught up in the whirl of life
  take no joy when they are not active.
They have to act;
they cannot control themselves.
They are prisoners in the world of illusion.
Never do they recover their right minds.
How unfortunate!

The above passage sounds remarkably hippie-like, does it not? If I should ever get around to writing my book, *Hippie Philosophy Through the Ages*, I will, of course, include much discussion of Chuangtse and Laotse.

Throughout classical Chinese period, poetry, painting, calligraphy and philosophy were all pretty much one and the same thing. One of the greatest of the Sung painters was Kuo Hsi (c. 1020-1090). I read somewhere that he never painted when he was in a lazy mood, because he believed that if one paints in a lazy mood, the painting will turn out weak. The following is a composite translation of a passage containing extremely interesting comments about Kuo Hsi by his son, Kuo Sze:

> On days when my father would paint,
> he would put his studio in order,
> take good care of his ink and brushes,
> settle himself by a bright window,
> compose his thoughts and begin.
> Sometimes he would leave his paintings
> unfinished for many days,
> because he wanted to avoid his lazy moods.

In many books on Chinese art, paintings are accompanied by poems. On the facing page is a landscape painting by Kuo Hsi followed by three additional landscape paintings of other Chinese artists.

Early Spring in the Mountains
Kuo Hsi (c. 1020-1090)

Landscape
Artist unknown (Southern Sung tradition)

Landscape
Tzu Yü (12th-13th centuries)

Landscape
Wang Tü (1748)

Continuing with poetry, here is one example of a remarkable poem by the 8th century poet Hanshan that goes hand-in-hand with paintings of old trees.

> Here is a tree as old as the forest itself.
> Its years of life cannot be measured.
> Its roots have seen the ravages of time.
> People laugh at its shoddy exterior
> Not knowing that beneath the bark
> Lies the core of truth!

Many Chinese poets have been known to be poets of idleness. *The Hall of Idleness* by Po Yüchien is especially well known:

> I'm too lazy to read the Taoist classics, for Tao
>   doesn't reside in books;
> Too lazy to look over the sutras, for they go no
>   deeper in Tao.
> The essence of Tao consists of a void,
>   cool and clear.
> But what is the void other than being the always
>   like a fool?
> I am even too lazy to read poetry, for when I
>   stop, the poetry is gone;
> Much too lazy to play the lute for music does
>   not last on the string.
> Too lazy to drink wine, for beyond the
>   drunkard's dream there are lakes and rivers.
> I'm too lazy to play chess, for besides the pawns

there are other things.
Too lazy to look at the hills and streams, for
   there is a painting within my very heart;
Too lazy to face wind and the moon, for within
   me is the dream of immortality.
Way too lazy to attend to worldly affairs,
   for inside me are all my possessions;
Too lazy to watch the changing of the seasons,
   for I have my own processions.
Pine trees may well decay and rot, but I shall
   never change!
Is it not fitting that this be called
   the Hall of Idleness?

Another prime example of an idleness poem is the *Lazy Man's Song* by the 8th century poet Po Chi-I:

I have an office, but am too lazy to use it.
I have land, but am too lazy to work it.
My house leaks, but I am too lazy to patch it.
My clothes are worn, but I am too lazy to
   mend them.
I am even too lazy to drink my wine!
It's as if my wine cup was empty.
I have a lute, but am too lazy too strum it.
It could just as well have no strings.
When told I have no more rice,
I am too lazy to grind some.
When I get letters from friends and relatives,
I am to lazy to open them;
They are too much if a bother!

I have been told that Hsi Shu-yeh passed his life
  in idleness,
But he played his lute and worked his forge.
He does not compare with me in idleness!

About his own poems, he writes:

Much laziness and idleness give me leisure.
How do I spend these idle days?
I cannot discard the inkstone and the brush.
Sometimes I compose a poem.
But my poems lack color and flavor,
A thing which people deride.
Some criticize the flatness of meter.
Others the plainness of word.

Po Chi-I was not only a great poet of leisure
and idleness, but also of quietude, serenity, and
meditation, as these poems reveal:

The Free Mind

I go to sleep as spontaneously as the birds fly
  back to the forest.
My mind is as free as that of a monk.
I am like a crane, crying under a pine tree.
I sit in the middle of the night,
And do not even answer calls from my daughter
  or wife.

The Illusion of Life

Ever since my days of childhood,
Until even now, when I am old,
My interests have changed over the years,
But the underlying principle is always the same.
Worldly ambition does not lead to
   self-realization.
Non-attachment alone is the path to truth.
However, an over-eagerness in the pursuit
   of truth,
Might indicate that one is still in the world
   of illusion.

One of the best known poets in China was the 9th century poet T'ao Chien (also known as T'ao Yuanming.) He was known as a perfect poet of leisure, idleness, and quietude. The following two poems are well known:

The Meaning of Things

I built a house away from men,
So as not to hear the noise of horse and carriage.
How is this done?
When the mind is free, my place is quiet.
I gather chrysanthemums beneath the
   Eastern hedges.
And I silently gaze at the beautiful mountains.
The mountain air is fresh in the evening sun.
And the birds flock together to return home.

In all these things there is deep meaning,
But when I try to express it, I cannot find words.

Once More Fields and Gardens

Even in my youth,
I was not in tune with worldly pleasures.
I preferred the rooted hills.
Such folly to spend one's life like fallen leaves!
Caught between the dust of city streets!
But I so lived for many years.
The caged bird longs for the fluttering
   of leaves.
The fish in the pool longs for the streams.
Migratory birds fly back to the streams in which
   they were hatched.
I have travelled the entire country,
And have finally come back to the fields of
   my childhood.
And my walled garden with its quiet paths.
My property is a little one of about ten acres.
My thatched house has eight or nine rooms.
On its North side, the eaves are overhung with
   fallen leaves of elm trees.
Willow trees break the forces of winds.
The village is not in sight.
A dog barks in the lane.
And a cock crows in the trees.
My courtyard has no dust or clutter.
Peace and quiet live in my rooms.
With the calm and leisure of the moon shining
   through the open door.
For many years I lived in a cage,

But now I have returned!
One must return,
If one is to fill one's nature.

These beautiful lines were written by Ch'eng Hao, another 9th century Chinese poet:

During the day, when the breeze is light,
I amble along the river amidst blooming trees.
People cannot understand my joy,
They say that I am loafing, like an idle man.

I love the following two lines by the famous Tang dynasty poet Li Tai Po:

You ask why I live in these blue mountains?
I smile but do not answer.

There is no poet I love more than Wang Wei (8th century.) He was known not only as the greatest poet-painter in China, but also as the greatest poet and the greatest painter in China. About himself as poet and painter, Wang Wei wrote:

After all these years,
I am too weary to compose poems.
Completely aware of my agedness
I am aware that people regard me
    as a poet.
But in some former life,

I must have been a painter
Since I am so inclined towards art!
Many consider me a painter,
But not for my pictures, only my name.
How very little they understand my true nature!

Unfortunately, I do not have any prints of Wang Wei's paintings. However, here are two examples of paintings done in the style of Wang Wei:

Paintings in the style of Wang Wei from a scroll entitled:
Clearing After Snowfall On the Mountain Along The River

Some of Wang Wei's most remarkable poems are very short ones which to an amazing degree recall to the reader's mind pre-conscious impressions. But for the reading of such poems, these pre-conscious impressions may never have arisen to a conscious level. The following seven poems exemplify what I have in mind:

South Hill

A small boat makes its way to South Hill
North Hill harder to reach—river too wide.
On the distant shore, I see families
  moving about
Too far to be recognized.

Deer Forest Hermitage

Through the deep woods, slanting rays
  of sunlight
Cast motley patterns on the floor.
No glimpse of man on these lonely mountains,
Yet faint voices drift in the air.

At the Rapids

Under the splatter of the rain,
The swirling waters glide over slippery stones.
Leaping waves dash each other.
The egret too frightened to dive for fish.

Middle Life

In the days of my middle life,
I am deeply immersed in the philosophy
  of the Tao.
Now I understand what is good and beautiful.

I recently came to live in the mountains
   of Chung-nan.
When I am happy, I roam the hills.
I roam alone, here and there.
When I come to the source of the stream,
I settle down and enjoy the rising mists.
I sometimes meet one who dwells in the woods.
We chat and laugh together,
And I do not want to go home!

Late in Life

Now, late in life, I understand the Doctrine of
   the Void:
Keep away from the swarming multitude!
I clean my cottage and prepare for the arrival of
   a monk.
He comes to me from distant mountains.
He descends from cloud-hidden peaks,
To see me in my simple home.
We sit in the grass and share the resin of
   the pine.
We burn incense and read the book of the Tao.
When the day is over, I light the lamp.
The temple bells announce the beginning
   of evening.
Finally, I experience the peace born
   of quietness.
The contemplative life blesses one with leisure.
Why should one think of returning?
The worldly life is empty and void!

Be Not Disquieted

Be not disquieted by kindness, insult, joy
　or sorrow.
If you rely on good or evil, you will only waste
your time...
Why seek advice from the Yellow Emperor
　or Confucius?
Who knows but that our lives are merely
　a dream?

In the Bamboo Grove

Sitting alone in the bamboo grove,
I strum the lute as I hum a tune.
No one knows I am here,
Save for the bright moon looking down on me.

Concerning our main theme of leisure, idleness, and quietude in this part of the book—and especially quietude—I can think of no lovelier ending for this section and for this entire work than Wang Wei's famous poem, *An Answer to Assistant Magistrate Chang*:

In my quiet evening years of life,
I am no longer a slave to the world's affairs.
I plan to retire to my old forest.
Where the wind will play
about my girdle.
And the moon will smile upon me

as I strum my lute.
You want to know what governs
failure and success?
Just listen to the fisherman's song
drifting from the river estuary.

Bibliography

Aristotle's Metaphysics. Ross, W. D., trans. 2 vols. Oxford: Clarendon Press, 1924.

Bierce, Ambrose. *The Devil's Dictionary.* New York: Doubleday, Page and Company, 1911.

Boswell, James. *Account of Corsica.* London: Edward and Charles Dilly, 1768.

_____. *Life of Johnson.* London: Everyman's Library, 1906.

Burroughs, John. *Literary Values.* Vol. X of *The Writings of John Burroughs.* Boston: Houghton, Mifflin and Company, 1902.

_____. *Heart of Burroughs' Journals,* Clara Barrus, ed. Boston: Houghton, and Mifflin Company, 1928.

Colman, George. *Random Records.* London, Henry Colburn and Richard Bentley, 1830.

De Grazia, Sebastian. *Of Time, Work and Leisure.* Garden City, NY: Anchor Books, Doubleday and Company, 1964.

The Dialogues of Plato. Jowett, B., trans. Vol. IV. London: Oxford University Press, 1892.

Fields, James T. *Yesterdays With Authors.* Boston: Houghton, Mifflin and Company, 1900.

Gibbon, Edward. *Autobiographies of Edward Gibbon.* John Murray, ed. London: J. Murray, 1896.

_____. *The Decline and Fall of the Roman Empire.* 7 vols. J. B. Bury, ed. London: Methuen, 1909-1914.

Hutton, Lawrence. *Talks In a Library.* New York: G. P. Putnam's Sons, 1905.

Johnson, Samuel. *The Rambler.* 3 vols. Liverpool: W. Robinson and Sons, 1826.

Lin, Yutang. *The Importance of Living*. New York: The John Day Company, 1937.

Mabie, Hamilton Wright. *Essays in Nature and Culture*. New York: Dodd, Mead, and Company, 1901.

_____. *My Study Fire*. New York, Dodd, Mead, and Company, 1897.

McCarthy, Justin. *Reminiscences*. New York: Harper & Brothers, 1899.

Mumby, Frank A. *The Romance of Bookselling*. Boston: Little, Brown and Company, 1911.

Newton, A. Edward. *The Amenities of Book Collecting*. Boston: Little, Brown and Company, 1918.

_____. *The Book Collecting Game*. Boston: Little, Brown and Company, 1928.

_____. *End Papers*. Boston: Little, Brown and Company, 1933.

_____. *The Greatest Book in the World*. Boston: Little, Brown and Company, 1925.

_____. *End Papers*. Boston: Little, Brown and Company, 1933.

_____. *Magnificent Farce*. Boston: Little, Brown and Company, 1912.

_____. *A Tourist in Spite of Himself*. Boston: Little, Brown and Company, 1930.

Repplier, Agnes. *Essays in Idleness*. Boston: Houghton, Mifflin and Company, 1894.

Rosenbach, A. S. W. *Books and Bidders*. Boston: Little, Brown, and Company, 1927.

Skinner, Otis. *Mad Folk of the Theatre*: *Ten Studies in Temperament* Indianapolis, IN: Bobbs-Merrill, 1928.

Spencer, Hazelton, Layman, Beverly J., and Ferry, David, eds. *British Literature*. 3rd ed. Lexington, MA: D. C. Heath, 1974.

Index

Account of Corsica
(Boswell), 59, 168
Active Life, The
(Chuangtse), 150
Allingham, William, 37
*Amenities of Book
Collecting, The*
(Newton), 78, 80, 96,
105, 169
*An Answer to Assistant
Magistrate Chang*
(Wang, Wei), 166
Aristotle, 52, 148, 168
At the Rapids (Wang,
Wei), 164
Austen, Jane, 5
*Autobiographies of
Edward Gibbon*
(Gibbon), 9, 60

Bankei, 74
Be Not Disquieted
(Wang, Wei), 166
Betterton, Thomas, 22
Bible
New Testament
translation, 107,
108. *See* also
Tyndale, William
Bierce, Ambrose, 5, 17,
19, 20, 168
*Book Collecting Game,
The* (Newton), 78,
169
Books and Bidders
(Rosenbach), 78, 97,
169
Booth, Junius Brutus,
28, 29, 30, 32
Boswell, James, 49-59,
62, 63, 77, 96, 111,
130, 131, 168
on literary fame, 59
Bright, John, 38, 39, 41,
43
British Literature, 3rd
ed. (Ferry), 126
Bronte sisters, 87, 88,
91
Browning, Robert, 37
Burroughs, John, 64, 67,
69, 70, 71, 75, 168
Journals, 71–73
Literary Values, 64–
67
Style and the Man,
67–69

Capitol Repertory
Theatre of Albany,

New York, 22
Carlyle, Thomas, 37,
    38, 130, 144
Ch'eng, Hao, 162
Charles II, King of
    England, 21, 24
Chatterton, Thomas
    literary forgeries,
        110, 112, 113
Chuangtse, 122, 123,
    141, 150, 151
*Clearing After Snowfall
    on the Mountain
    Along the River I*,
    163
*Clearing After Snowfall
    on the Mountain
    Along the River II*,
    163
Cooke, George
    Frederick, 28- 31
Coolidge, Calvin, 17
counterfeiter court case,
    89–91
Critique of Pure Reason
    (Kant), 5
Crutch, Joseph Wood
    on Thomas Gray,
        126

Dailey Meditations
    (Paine), 102
*Decline and Fall of the
    Roman Empire, The*
    (Gibbon), 60, 62, 168

Deer Forest Hermitage
    (Wang, Wei), 164
Devil, 16, 17, 168
Devil's Dictionary, The
    (Bierce), 17, 168
Dialogues of Plato, The
    (Plato), 146, 168
Dickens, Charles, 37,
    39, 88, 91, 93
Doyle, Sir Arthur
    Conan, 114–15

*Early Spring in the
    Mountains* (Kuo,
    Hsi), 153
Eliot Indian Bible, 102
Emerson, Ralph Waldo,
    9, 139, 140
    on luck, 85
Emperor Julian, 149
End Papers (Newton),
    78, 87, 129, 169
English Dictionary, The
    (Johnson), 52
Essaies (Bacon), 97
Essays in Idleness
    (Repplier), 129, 169
*Essays in Nature and
    Culture* (Mabie), 139

Folger Shakespeare
    Library, 100
forgeries
    literary, 109–13
Franklin, Benjamin, 84

Free Mind, The (Po, Chi-I), 159

Gibbon, Edward, 60-62, 168
  on literary fame, 60–61
Goethe, Johann Wolfgang von, 58
Goldsmith, Oliver, 40, 56
Gray, Thomas, 9, 113, 126, 127
Greatest Book in the World, The (Newton), 78, 169
Gwinn, Nell, 24-26

Hall of Idleness, The (Po, Yüchien), 157
Han-shan, 157
Harrison, Frederic
  on writing style, 68
Hazlitt, William
  on Thomas Gray, 9, 126, 127
Heart of Burroughs' Journals, The (Burroughs), 71, 168
Hippie Philosophy Through the Ages (Smullyan), 151
Horney, Karen, 122
Houdini, Harry, 113–15
Huang, Po, 74

Hume, David, 60
Hunt, Leigh, 83, 84
Hutton, Lawrence, 12, 13, 15, 168

Illusion of Life, The (Po, Chi-I), 160
Importance of Living, The (Lin, Yutang), 6, 169
"In Praise of Idleness," (Russell) 123
In the Bamboo Grove (Wang, Wei), 166
Ireland, William Henry
  literary forgeries, 110-112

Johnson, Samuel, 9, 46, 47, 49, 50-59, 61-63, 77, 78, 80, 83, 96, 102, 129-131, 168
  on idleness, 51
jokes
  atomic scientists, 86
  bartender, 109
  fugue, 19
  little boy at piano, 19
Jordan, Dora, 25, 27, 28, 111

Kant, Immanuel, 5, 35
Kean, Edmund, 28, 29, 30, 31
Keller, Helen, 12, 13, 15

King Lear
   (Shakespeare), 30, 33
Kuo, Hsi, 152, 153
Kuo, Sze, 152

Landscape, 154
Landscape (Tzu, Yü),
   155
Landscape (Wang, Tü),
   156
Laotse, 143, 151
Late in Life (Wang,
   Wei), 165
Lexington Theatre, 22
Li, Tai Po, 162
Life of Johnson
   (Boswell), 49
Lin, Yutang, 6–8
Lincoln, Abraham, 6,
   12, 69
Lloyd, Sam
   magic trick, 115,
      116, 119
Lucillius, 149
luck, 85, 86
   Chinese story, 86

Mabie, Hamilton
   Wright, 138, 139,
   141, 142, 144, 145,
   169
   essay on "Repose",
      139–41
   essay on "Solitude
      and Silence",
141–42
   essay on "Unhasting,
      Unresting, 142–44
   essay on idleness,
      144–45
Magnificent Farce, A
   (Newton), 78, 82, 83,
   169
mathematician, 38, 48,
   141
mathematics, 12, 20, 47,
   136
Mathews, Charles, 34-
   36
McCarthy, Justin, 33,
   35, 37, 38, 169
Meaning of Things, The
   (T'ao, Chien), 160
Metaphysics (Aristotle),
   148, 168
Middle Life (Wang,
   Wei), 164

Newton, A. Edward, 77-
   91, 96, 97, 98, 101,
   129, 135, 169
   counterfeiter court
      case observer, 89–
      91
   love of book
      collecting, 82
   on being a
      bibliophile, 78
   on Bernard Quaritch,
      105

on luck, 85

O'Henry, 103
Of Time, Work, and Leisure (de Grazia), 147
Once More Fields and Gardens (T'ao, Chien), 161

Paradise Lost (Milton), 42, 66
Pepys, Samuel, 84
Pilgrim's Progress (Bunyan), 101, 102
Po, Chi-I, 158, 159
Po, Yüchien, 157

Quaritch, Alfred, 104
Quaritch, Bernard, 104-106

Rambler, The (Johnson), 49, 168
Rand, Ayn, 85
Random Records (Colman), 61, 168
Reminiscences (McCarthy), 33, 37, 169
Repplier, Agnes, 129-131, 133, 135-137, 169
  essay on Samuel Johnson, 129–31

  on Charles Lamb, 138
  on Horace, 133–34
  on Montaigne, 132
  on Sir Walter Scott, 137
  on the "Gospel of Work", 132
  on Voltaire, 131
Reynolds, Sir Joshua, 50, 56
Richard III (Shakespeare), 29-32
Rosenbach, Dr. A. S. W., 78, 97-101-104, 107, 109-111, 113, 169
Russell, Bertrand
  on guilt, 84
  on idleness, 123
  on work, 125

Seneca, 149
Shakespeare, William, 16, 30, 41, 42, 65, 66, 98, 100, 110, 111
Sin, 17
Skinner, Otis, 21, 22, 24, 28, 29, 169
  love of book collecting, 82
Smullyan, Raymond M.
  favorite Twain anecdote, 16
  on "discipline" in

education, 47–49
on acting theories, 21
on being a carnival
    worker, 23
on sleep and
    longevity, 134
on work and leisure,
    125–28
personal library
    philosophy of, 79
Socrates, 146, 147
South Hill (Wang,Wei),
    164
Studio Ensemble
    Company of New
    York, 23
swindles
    advertising, 118
    joking, 119
    Poe, Edgar Allen,
        116
    *ten-dollar bar
        swindle*, 117

T'ao, Chien, 160
T'ao, Yuanming. *See*
    T'ao, Chien
Tao, 143
Taoist, 126, 141
Taoistic, 139, 141, 144,
    148
Tennyson, Alfred
    (Lord), 37
Thackeray, William
    Makepeace, 37, 39,

40, 91- 95
as lecturer, 92–94
Theodorus, 146, 147
Thoreau, Henry David,
    9, 139
*Tourist In Spite of
    Himself, A* (Newton),
    78
Twain, Mark, 5, 6, 13,
    15-17, 45
on eternal
    punishment, 48
on opera, 13
on Richard Wagner,
    13
on the German
    Language, 13
Tyndale, William, 107,
    108

Vicar of Wakefield
    (Goldsmith), 40
Voltaire, 68, 131
Vortigern and Rowena
    literary forgeries,
    111. *See also*
    Ireland, William
    Henry

Wagner, Richard, 13, 16
Walpole, Horace, 113
Wang, Wei, 162–67
Whitman, Walt, 6, 9,
    139
on duties, 83

Widener, Harry Elkins,
    96, 97
*Writings of John
    Burroughs, The*
    (Burroughs), 64, 168
Wu Wei, 133, 141, 143

Yesterdays With

Authors, Fields,
    James T., 92, 168

Zen, 74
Zen-master
    Bankei, 74
    Huang Po, 74